The Successful Reseller's Roadmap

A Comprehensive Guide to Thriving in the Reselling Industry

Written by: Sayed Aris Khelwati

"GROWTH AND COMFORT NEVER COEXIST"

Ginni Rometty | CEO of IBM

Table of Contents

From Kandahar to Canada: My Journey of Resilience and Aspiration 4

    Introduction: 7

    Chapter 1: Understanding the Reseller Market 9

    1. Market Research and Analysis 9
    2. Identifying Target Audience 10
    3. Competitive Analysis 12
    4. Understanding Market Dynamics 15
    5. Setting Realistic Goals 17

    Chapter 2: Finding the Right Products 20

    1. Identifying Trends and Opportunities 20
    2. Evaluating Product Viability 22
    3. Testing Product Ideas 24
    4. Product Diversification 26
    5. Building a Unique Selling Proposition (USP) 28

    Chapter 3: Sourcing and Supplier Relationships 32

    1. Finding Reliable Suppliers 32
    2. Negotiating Terms and Prices 35
    3. Quality Control and Assurance 37
    4. Building Long-Term Supplier Relationships 40
    5. Diversifying Supply Chain 43

    Chapter 4: Marketing and Branding 46

    1. Creating a Brand Identity 47
    2. Developing a Marketing Strategy 49
    3. Content Marketing and SEO 53
    4. Social Media Marketing 57
    5. Email Marketing and Customer Retention 61

    Chapter 5: Sales Techniques and Strategies 65

1. Understanding the Sales Funnel..65
2. Lead Generation Techniques..68
3. Effective Sales Pitches..71
4. Closing Sales and Overcoming Objections 74

Chapter 6: Customer Relationship Management 77
1. Understanding Customer Needs and Preferences 77
2. Personalizing Customer Interactions......................................79
3. Omni-channel Engagement...82
4. Proactive Customer Support 84
5. Feedback and Improvement 86

Chapter 7: Optimizing Operations and Efficiency 88
1. Inventory Management Best Practices..................................88
2. Streamlining Order Fulfillment 91

Chapter 8: Financial Management and Profitability 94
1. Budgeting and Financial Planning 94
2. Cash Flow Optimization 96
3. Cost Control and Expense Management...............................97
4. Pricing Strategy and Profit Margins.......................................97
5. Financial Performance Analysis..97

Chapter 9: Scaling Your Reselling Business 99
1. Market Expansion Strategies 99
2. Diversifying Product Portfolio 99
3. E-commerce and Digital Transformation 100
4. Operational Scalability and Infrastructure........................100
5. Strategic Partnerships and Alliances 100

Conclusion...102

From Kandahar to Canada: My Journey of Resilience and Aspiration

My name is Sayed Aris Khelwati, an Afghan who embarked on a journey to Canada a year ago, fueled by dreams and a determination to build a future beyond the ordinary. My life in Kandahar was marked by a series of jobs that, while varied, served the purpose of providing for my family. I worked in roles that ranged from administering vaccinations to labor work, teaching, handling administrative duties, securing the airport, and contributing to NGOs. Each job, in its own way, was a blessing—especially in a country where opportunities were scarce. I thanked Allah every day for the chance to work when so many others struggled to find employment. But deep down, I knew I wanted more. I longed to do something significant, something that would leave a lasting impact.

Ever since I was a child, Canada held a special place in my heart. It was the land of dreams, a place I always envisioned as the destination where I would build my future. However, life took me on a different path initially. I sought advice from one of my expatriate managers, Mr. Hanif Mulla, a wise and experienced man from the UK. He advised me to go to Dubai, a bustling hub of opportunity, where I could work hard, save money, and eventually start my own business. It sounded like the perfect plan. I made several attempts to secure a visa for Dubai, driven by the hope of following his advice. A friend I knew only through WhatsApp tried to help me with the visa process, but each attempt ended in disappointment. The reality of holding an Afghan passport made the process extraordinarily challenging.

Just when I thought my dreams of a better life might remain unfulfilled, a new opportunity emerged. In 2023, I received an unexpected email from the IRCC, informing me that my application to immigrate to Canada, which I had submitted in August 2021, was progressing. What had seemed like an unattainable dream was now within reach. In a matter of months, I found myself in Pakistan to complete the application process. After two long months, the day finally arrived when I boarded a flight to Halifax, Canada, on September 20, 2023. Stepping onto Canadian soil felt surreal—a childhood dream had come true.

Arriving in Canada was not the end of my journey but the beginning of a new chapter. I had always been fascinated by the world of sales and marketing, particularly with the idea of becoming an Amazon FBA reseller. Back in Afghanistan, this ambition was almost impossible to pursue due to numerous challenges. But now, in Canada, I was determined to make it a reality. My first opportunity came through a friend named Zeeshan, who owned a mobile accessories kiosk. He took me under his wing, allowing me to work with him and learn the intricacies of sales. The experience was invaluable, and it laid the foundation for my future endeavors.

Eager to expand my knowledge, I enrolled in courses offered by Workplace Education Nova Scotia and the Strait Area Chamber of Commerce, where I had the privilege of learning from incredible mentors like Georges Hanna and Rick McMullen. The Immigrant Services Association of Nova Scotia (ISANS) supported me in accessing these courses and taking the first steps in my business journey. Their guidance helped me refine my skills in sales and marketing, giving me the confidence to pursue my dreams. However, before I could fully immerse myself in the world of reselling, I faced another challenge—there was no comprehensive guide or book on the subject that I could find. It was a frustrating realization, but one that eventually led to a breakthrough.

During one of our classes, Georges Hanna suggested to the entire group that writing and publishing a book on Amazon KDP could be an excellent way to share our knowledge and experiences. This advice resonated with many of us, and the idea of creating a resource for aspiring resellers began to take shape. The encouragement to write a book planted a seed that would eventually grow into "The Successful Reseller's Roadmap." After months of hard work, research, and writing, the book was finally published on August 1st, 2024. It stands not just as a guide but as a testament to our collective journey—a roadmap for anyone striving to turn their dreams into reality.

But this is just the beginning. My story continues, as I pursue new goals, take on new challenges, and strive to make an even greater impact. The road ahead is long, and I'm excited to see where it leads.

Introduction:

Tip: "Success in reselling starts with understanding the market, identifying the right products, and building strong customer relationships."

In this book, we will embark on a comprehensive journey to becoming a successful reseller. Our exploration will delve into every essential aspect of the reselling business, guiding you from the foundational steps of understanding the market dynamics to the advanced strategies necessary for scaling your business to new heights. Each chapter has been meticulously crafted to offer practical strategies that are not only grounded in sound theoretical frameworks but also tested and proven in real-world scenarios.

We will cover a wide range of topics, including market research, inventory management, marketing, customer relationship management, and financial planning. Through a blend of detailed analysis, real-world examples, and actionable insights, you will acquire the knowledge and tools needed to navigate the complexities of the reselling industry. The real-world examples provided will illustrate how successful resellers have overcome challenges and seized opportunities, offering you a blueprint for your own success.

This book is designed to cater to a diverse audience, whether you are a novice entrepreneur taking your first steps into the reselling world or an experienced reseller looking to expand and optimize your operations. For beginners, we provide clear, step-by-step guidance on how to establish a strong foundation for your business, including identifying profitable niches and building a solid brand identity. For seasoned resellers, we delve into advanced tactics for scaling your business, exploring new markets, and leveraging digital tools for growth.

Our goal is to make your journey through this book not only informative but also engaging and rewarding. We aim to equip you with the confidence and competence to tackle the challenges of the reselling industry head-on. As you progress through the chapters, you will gain a deeper understanding of the critical factors that influence success in reselling, and how you can apply this knowledge to achieve your business goals.

Ultimately, this book is your comprehensive guide to thriving in the reselling industry. We invite you to immerse yourself in the content, take actionable steps, and embrace the journey towards becoming a successful reseller. Whether your aim is to build a side hustle or a full-fledged enterprise, the insights and strategies provided here will be invaluable in helping you navigate and excel in this dynamic and ever-evolving market.

Chapter 1: Understanding the Reseller Market

Tip: "Knowing your market is the first step to becoming a successful reseller."

1. **Market Research and Analysis**

Conducting thorough market research and analysis is a foundational step for any successful reseller. This process involves a deep dive into understanding the landscape of your chosen market, identifying key trends, and recognizing the factors that influence consumer behavior. It's not just about knowing what products are currently popular; it's about predicting what will be in demand in the future and positioning your business accordingly.

For instance, if you are a reseller specializing in tech gadgets, it is essential to stay informed about emerging technologies and innovations. A thorough analysis might reveal a growing consumer interest in smart home devices, such as voice-activated assistants, smart thermostats, and automated lighting systems. This insight allows you to capitalize on the trend early, ensuring that your inventory includes the latest and most sought-after products.

Understanding consumer preferences and demand patterns also involves looking at demographic data, economic indicators, and cultural trends. Are younger consumers driving the demand for certain gadgets? Is there a shift towards eco-friendly or energy-efficient products? By answering these questions, you can tailor your product offerings to align with the values and preferences of your target audience.

Furthermore, market research isn't a one-time task; it's an ongoing process. The tech industry, for example, is characterized by rapid changes and continuous innovation. New products and technologies emerge regularly, and consumer preferences can shift quickly. Staying ahead of these changes requires constant monitoring and analysis. This might involve keeping up with industry news, attending trade shows, engaging with customers through surveys, and analyzing sales data to spot emerging trends.

By conducting comprehensive market research and analysis, you not only make informed business decisions but also reduce risks. You can avoid overstocking unpopular items and instead invest in products that have a high probability of success. This proactive approach helps you stay competitive, meet the evolving needs of your audience, and ultimately drive higher sales and profitability. In essence, a well-executed market research strategy is key to understanding your market and ensuring your business's growth and sustainability in the competitive landscape.

2. Identifying Target Audience

Defining your target audience is a critical step in creating a successful business strategy, as it allows you to tailor your marketing efforts and product offerings to meet the specific needs and preferences of potential customers.

This process involves a thorough analysis of various demographic factors, interests, and buying behaviors, which are essential for effectively reaching and engaging your ideal customer base.

To begin with, demographic factors such as age, gender, income level, education, and geographic location provide a foundational understanding of who your customers are. For instance, a fashion reseller targeting young professionals would focus on individuals in their 20s to 30s who are likely to have disposable income and are in need of stylish, affordable office wear. By identifying these characteristics, you can narrow down your marketing efforts to appeal specifically to this demographic, rather than casting a wide, unfocused net.

In addition to demographics, understanding the interests and lifestyles of your target audience is crucial. This involves considering their hobbies, values, and the type of content they consume. For the fashion reseller example, young professionals might value convenience and style, and be influenced by fashion trends they see on social media platforms like Instagram and Pinterest. They may also prioritize quality and affordability, looking for versatile pieces that can transition from the office to social settings. By aligning your product selection and marketing messaging with these interests, you can more effectively capture their attention and encourage them to engage with your brand.

Another key aspect is analyzing buying behaviors, which includes understanding how your target audience makes purchasing decisions. This can involve factors such as preferred shopping channels (online vs. in-store), payment preferences, and sensitivity to price changes or promotions. For instance, young professionals may prefer shopping online due to their busy schedules and might respond well to promotions such as discounts or bundle offers. By recognizing these preferences, you can optimize your sales strategies to meet their needs, such as offering an easy-to-navigate e-commerce site, flexible payment options, and occasional sales events.

Moreover, defining your target audience allows for more personalized marketing strategies. Personalization can significantly increase customer engagement and conversion rates. For example, you could use targeted ads on social media platforms, email marketing campaigns featuring curated content based on past purchases, or influencer partnerships that align with the interests of your audience. By delivering tailored content and products, you create a more relevant and engaging experience for your customers, which can lead to increased loyalty and repeat business.

Identifying and understanding your target audience is foundational to your business's success. It not only informs product development and inventory decisions but also guides your marketing strategies, ensuring that your messaging resonates with the right people. By focusing on the specific needs, preferences, and behaviors of your target market, you can build stronger connections with your customers, differentiate your brand, and ultimately drive higher sales and growth.

3. Competitive Analysis

Conducting a thorough competitive analysis is crucial for identifying opportunities and differentiating your business in a crowded marketplace. This process involves a systematic evaluation of your competitors' strengths and weaknesses, which helps you understand the competitive landscape and identify areas where your business can excel. By analyzing what your competitors are doing well and where they may be lacking, you can develop strategies to differentiate your offerings and create a unique value proposition.

To start, it's important to identify who your main competitors are. These can include both direct competitors (those selling similar products) and indirect competitors (those offering alternative solutions to the same customer needs). For instance, if you are a reseller of fitness equipment, your direct competitors would be other businesses selling similar gym equipment, while indirect competitors might include companies offering fitness apps or online workout subscriptions.

Once you've identified your competitors, the next step is to evaluate their strengths. This includes looking at their product range, pricing strategies, marketing tactics, customer service, brand reputation, and online presence. Understanding these elements can provide insights into why customers might choose their products over yours. For example, a competitor might have a strong online presence with a well-optimized e-commerce website, engaging social media channels, and a large customer base. They might also offer competitive pricing and a wide range of products, making them a go-to destination for customers.

Equally important is identifying your competitors' weaknesses. These are areas where they may be underperforming or failing to meet customer expectations. For instance, the reseller of fitness equipment might observe that their competitors have a reputation for poor customer service, such as slow response times, inadequate after-sales support, or a lack of detailed product information. This presents an opportunity for your business to differentiate itself by offering superior customer service. By providing timely and helpful responses, detailed product guides, and robust after-sales support, you can attract customers who prioritize these aspects.

Another critical aspect of competitive analysis is examining the market positioning and branding of your competitors. How do they position themselves in the market? What are their brand values and messaging? Understanding these elements can help you carve out a unique niche for your brand. For example, if most competitors are focusing on high-end, premium fitness equipment, there may be an opportunity to target budget-conscious consumers with affordable yet high-quality alternatives.

Competitive analysis also involves staying updated on your competitors' innovations and changes in strategies. This could include new product launches, changes in pricing, marketing campaigns, or expansions into new markets. Keeping an eye on these developments allows you to anticipate market trends and adjust your strategies accordingly.

A comprehensive competitive analysis not only helps you identify opportunities to improve and differentiate your offerings but also informs your strategic decisions. By understanding what your competitors are doing well and where they are falling short, you can tailor your business strategies to meet customer needs more effectively. This can include offering better customer service, more competitive pricing, unique product features, or a superior shopping experience. Ultimately, this analysis enables you to build a stronger brand, attract more customers, and achieve a sustainable competitive advantage in the market.

4. Understanding Market Dynamics

Staying competitive and responsive in the reselling business requires a deep understanding of market dynamics. This involves continuously monitoring and adapting to a variety of factors, including industry trends, regulatory changes, and technological advancements. By staying informed, you can make strategic decisions that keep your business relevant and appealing to your target audience.

One key aspect of understanding market dynamics is keeping up with industry news. This includes monitoring reports on market trends, consumer behavior shifts, and economic conditions that may impact demand for certain products. For instance, a reseller in the electronics market should pay close attention to trends in consumer electronics, such as the increasing interest in smart home devices, wearable technology, or advancements in artificial intelligence. By staying informed about these trends, you can anticipate changes in consumer demand and adjust your inventory and marketing strategies accordingly.

Regulatory updates are another critical component of market dynamics. Regulations can impact everything from product standards and safety requirements to import/export laws and taxation. For example, if new regulations are introduced that affect the import of electronic goods, a reseller must quickly adapt by ensuring compliance to avoid penalties and maintain smooth operations. Keeping abreast of these changes helps you mitigate risks and maintain a competitive edge.

Technological advancements also play a significant role in shaping market dynamics. The rapid pace of innovation in technology can lead to the introduction of new products and the obsolescence of others. For a reseller in the electronics market, it is crucial to monitor new product releases, emerging technologies, and shifts in consumer preferences. For example, if there is a surge in demand for the latest generation of smartphones or wearable fitness trackers, staying updated allows you to stock these trending items, attracting tech-savvy consumers looking for the latest gadgets. Additionally, advancements in logistics and e-commerce technology can offer new ways to improve your operations, such as adopting more efficient inventory management systems or enhancing your online shopping experience with better website features and customer service tools.

Moreover, understanding market dynamics involves analyzing competitive actions and market saturation. If a particular product category becomes oversaturated, with many competitors offering similar items, you may need to differentiate your offerings or explore new product categories to stay ahead. Conversely, identifying a gap in the market where demand is high but supply is limited can present a lucrative opportunity for expansion.

Understanding and adapting to market dynamics is essential for maintaining competitiveness in the reselling industry. It enables you to anticipate changes, capitalize on emerging opportunities, and navigate challenges. By staying informed about industry news, regulatory updates, and technological advancements, you can ensure that your business remains agile, responsive, and aligned with the needs and preferences of your target market. This proactive approach not only helps in maintaining a relevant and appealing product inventory but also positions your business for long-term success in a dynamic and ever-evolving market landscape.

5. Setting Realistic Goals

Setting realistic and specific goals is a fundamental practice for driving growth and measuring success in the reselling business. Clear objectives provide direction, focus efforts, and enable you to track progress, ensuring that your business remains on a strategic path toward achieving its long-term vision.

To begin, it is essential to establish goals that are Specific, Measurable, Achievable, Relevant, and Time-bound (SMART). This framework helps in crafting well-defined targets that can guide decision-making and operational activities. For example, instead of a vague goal like "increase sales," a SMART goal would be "increase sales by 20% in the next quarter through targeted marketing campaigns." This goal is specific (focused on sales increase), measurable (quantified by 20%), achievable (based on past performance and market analysis), relevant (aligned with business growth objectives), and time-bound (set for the next quarter).

Setting specific objectives allows you to concentrate your resources and efforts on activities that directly contribute to achieving these goals. For instance, if the goal is to increase sales, this might involve launching new marketing initiatives, improving customer service, expanding product offerings, or optimizing the e-commerce experience. Each of these actions can be aligned with the overarching objective, ensuring a cohesive and focused approach.

Measurable goals are crucial for tracking progress and assessing the effectiveness of your strategies. By having clear metrics, such as sales numbers, website traffic, conversion rates, or customer satisfaction scores, you can monitor your performance over time. This quantitative data provides valuable insights into what is working well and what needs adjustment. For example, if a reseller aims to boost sales through targeted marketing campaigns, they can track metrics such as ad click-through rates, sales from specific campaigns, and return on investment (ROI) to gauge success.

Achievability is another critical component of goal-setting. Goals should be challenging yet attainable, taking into account the current market conditions, available resources, and business capabilities. Setting overly ambitious goals can lead to frustration and demotivation if they are not met, while setting goals that are too easy may not drive the necessary effort and innovation. It is important to strike a balance that encourages growth and improvement without setting up the business for failure.

Relevance ensures that the goals are aligned with your overall business strategy and mission. This alignment is vital for ensuring that all efforts are contributing to the long-term vision of the company. For example, if a reseller's long-term strategy is to become a leading provider of eco-friendly products, their goals should reflect this focus, such as increasing the percentage of sustainable products in their inventory or improving brand positioning in the eco-friendly market segment.

Finally, having time-bound goals creates a sense of urgency and a clear timeframe for achievement. This encourages consistent effort and regular evaluation of progress. Setting quarterly, monthly, or even weekly targets can help in maintaining momentum and adjusting strategies as needed.

Setting realistic and well-defined goals is a key component of effective business management. It provides a roadmap for success, guiding strategic decisions and operational actions. By focusing on specific, measurable, achievable, relevant, and time-bound objectives, you can drive meaningful progress, track your achievements, and continually align your efforts with your business's long-term goals. This disciplined approach not only facilitates growth and success but also enables you to respond proactively to challenges and opportunities in the dynamic reselling market.

Call to Action:
Research and define your target market, competitors, and set realistic business goals.

Activity:
Conduct a SWOT analysis (Strengths, Weaknesses, Opportunities, Threats) of your reselling business.

Chapter 2: Finding the Right Products

Tip: "Choose products that not only meet market demand but also align with your business strengths."

1. Identifying Trends and Opportunities

In the ever-evolving reselling industry, staying ahead of trends and capitalizing on emerging opportunities is essential for maintaining a competitive edge. This process involves actively monitoring the market to identify shifts in consumer preferences, emerging product categories, and new market niches. Utilizing a range of tools and resources, such as Google Trends, social media analytics, and industry reports, can provide valuable insights into what's gaining traction among consumers.

Google Trends is an invaluable tool for tracking the popularity of search terms over time. By analyzing search data, you can gain insights into rising interests and seasonal trends. For example, a home décor reseller might use Google Trends to discover that searches for "eco-friendly home decor" are on the rise. This indicates a growing consumer preference for sustainable and environmentally friendly products, suggesting a potential area for inventory expansion. By aligning your product offerings with these emerging interests, you can attract eco-conscious customers and differentiate your brand in a crowded market.

Social media platforms also serve as a rich source of real-time data on consumer trends and behaviors. Platforms like Instagram, Pinterest, and TikTok are especially useful for visual industries, as they highlight trending aesthetics, popular styles, and influential products. Monitoring hashtags, influencer content, and user-generated posts can reveal emerging trends and popular items. For example, if a particular style of minimalist furniture is frequently featured in influencer posts and garnering high engagement, this could indicate a growing trend. By incorporating such products into your inventory, you can tap into this trend and meet the evolving tastes of your audience.

Industry reports and market research publications provide comprehensive analyses of market trends, competitive landscapes, and consumer behavior. These reports often include data on market size, growth forecasts, and key drivers influencing the industry. By reviewing these insights, you can identify broader market trends and anticipate future shifts. For instance, a report indicating a projected increase in the demand for smart home technology could prompt a reseller to explore related product lines, such as smart lighting, security systems, or voice-activated assistants.

Recognizing and capitalizing on these trends early is crucial for maintaining relevance and competitiveness. It allows you to adapt your product offerings to meet current consumer demands and preferences, ensuring that your inventory remains appealing to your target audience. Moreover, staying attuned to trends can help you identify gaps in the market, where consumer demand is not yet fully met. This can provide opportunities to introduce innovative products or niche offerings that set your business apart from competitors.

Identifying trends and opportunities is a proactive and strategic approach to business growth. By leveraging tools like Google Trends, social media analytics, and industry reports, you can stay informed about emerging consumer preferences and market dynamics. This foresight enables you to make informed decisions about inventory management, marketing strategies, and product development. By continuously adapting to the changing landscape, you can position your business for sustained success and growth in the reselling industry.

2. Evaluating Product Viability

Evaluating product viability is a critical process in the reselling business, as it determines whether a product is worth investing in and whether it has the potential to generate a profitable return. This comprehensive evaluation involves assessing several key factors, including market demand, competition, and profit margins. By thoroughly analyzing these aspects, you can make informed decisions that minimize risks and optimize profitability.

Assessing Market Demand is the first step in evaluating product viability. This involves researching whether there is a sufficient consumer interest in the product. Understanding market demand helps you estimate the potential sales volume and revenue. Tools like Google Trends, keyword research, and market research reports can provide valuable insights into consumer interest levels. For instance, if a reseller is considering selling ergonomic office chairs, they would first examine search trends and consumer discussions to gauge how popular these products are. High demand suggests a strong potential for sales, making the product a viable addition to your inventory.

Identifying Key Competitors is another crucial aspect of product viability evaluation. Analyzing the competitive landscape helps you understand the market saturation and the strengths and weaknesses of existing players. This analysis includes identifying who the main competitors are, what they offer, and how they price their products. It also involves understanding their market positioning, customer reviews, and overall market share. For example, if numerous established brands dominate the market for ergonomic office chairs, a reseller must consider how they can differentiate their offerings, perhaps through unique features, better customer service, or competitive pricing. Understanding the competition helps in strategizing how to position your products effectively and carve out a niche in the market.

Calculating Profit Margins is essential to ensure the product can be sold at a price that covers costs and generates a profit. This calculation involves considering all costs associated with sourcing, storing, and selling the product, including manufacturing costs, shipping, taxes, and any other overhead expenses. Once these costs are accounted for, you can determine a pricing strategy that not only attracts customers but also ensures a healthy profit margin. For example, after accounting for all expenses, a reseller might determine that selling ergonomic office chairs at a specific price point will yield a sufficient profit margin. It's important to ensure that the selling price is competitive while still allowing for a satisfactory profit.

Evaluating Additional Factors such as product lifecycle, seasonality, and legal considerations is also part of the viability assessment. Products with a long lifecycle or those that can be sold year-round offer more stable revenue opportunities. Seasonal products, on the other hand, may require more strategic planning for inventory management and marketing. Additionally, understanding any legal or regulatory requirements, such as safety standards or import regulations, is crucial to avoid potential compliance issues.

Evaluating product viability is a multi-faceted process that involves a detailed examination of market demand, competition, and profit margins. By conducting a thorough analysis, you can make informed decisions about which products to add to your inventory, ensuring that you invest in items that are likely to be profitable. This careful assessment helps minimize risks, optimize resources, and ultimately, maximize profits in the reselling business. By consistently evaluating product viability, you can adapt to market changes, stay competitive, and achieve sustainable growth.

3. Testing Product Ideas

Testing product ideas on a smaller scale is a prudent and effective strategy for resellers to assess potential market success without committing to significant investments upfront. This approach allows you to gather essential data on consumer interest, product performance, and overall feasibility. By conducting limited-time offers or small-scale tests, you can minimize risks, refine your product offerings, and make informed decisions before scaling up.

Conducting Limited-Time Offers is a practical method for testing new products. By introducing a product for a short period, you can create a sense of urgency and exclusivity, which can drive customer interest and purchases. This tactic not only helps gauge immediate consumer response but also allows you to assess the effectiveness of your marketing strategies. For example, a tech reseller might launch a new gadget as part of a limited-time promotion, offering a discount or a bundle deal. The sales data and customer feedback collected during this period can provide valuable insights into the product's appeal and market demand. If the product performs well, it indicates a potential for broader market success, while a lukewarm response may suggest the need for adjustments or reevaluation.

Small-Scale Tests involve introducing a limited quantity of a new product to your inventory. This approach helps you evaluate logistics, supply chain capabilities, and inventory management processes. By starting with a small batch, you can monitor the entire supply chain from procurement to sales, identifying any challenges or bottlenecks that may arise. For instance, a tech reseller testing a new line of gadgets can monitor the efficiency of the shipping and handling process, customer service inquiries, and the rate of returns or exchanges. This trial phase allows you to fine-tune your operations and ensure that you can handle larger volumes if the product proves successful.

Gathering Customer Feedback is a critical component of testing product ideas. Engaging with customers who purchase the test products provides direct insights into their experiences, preferences, and potential concerns. Encouraging reviews, surveys, and direct feedback helps you understand the strengths and weaknesses of the product. For example, a tech reseller might ask customers to rate their experience with the new gadget, focusing on aspects such as usability, functionality, and overall satisfaction. This feedback is invaluable for making informed adjustments to the product or its marketing strategy, ensuring it better meets customer expectations.

Validating Product Ideas through testing helps build confidence in the product's market viability. By analyzing the data collected from limited-time offers, small-scale tests, and customer feedback, you can make evidence-based decisions about whether to fully invest in the product. This process helps mitigate the risk of overstocking or investing heavily in products that may not perform well. Additionally, testing allows you to refine your product selection, marketing strategies, and pricing models, optimizing them for a broader market launch.

Testing product ideas is a crucial step in the reselling process, allowing you to validate potential products before committing to large-scale investments. By leveraging limited-time offers, small-scale tests, and customer feedback, you can gather essential data, minimize risks, and make informed decisions. This approach not only helps ensure the success of new product launches but also supports sustainable growth and profitability in the reselling business. Through careful testing and evaluation, you can confidently expand your product offerings, knowing that you are meeting market demand and consumer expectations.

4. Product Diversification

Product diversification is a strategic approach that involves expanding your product range to address a broader array of customer needs and preferences. This strategy not only helps in attracting different customer segments but also plays a crucial role in mitigating risks and enhancing overall business resilience. By offering a diverse selection of products, you create multiple revenue streams, reduce dependency on a single product category, and position your business for long-term growth.

Expanding Product Offerings allows you to tap into new market segments and cater to a wider audience. For instance, a beauty products reseller who initially specializes in skincare can broaden their inventory to include haircare and makeup items. This diversification helps in capturing the interest of customers who may have different beauty needs and preferences, thereby increasing the potential for sales and revenue. By addressing various aspects of personal care, you not only enhance the customer experience but also position your business as a one-stop-shop for a range of beauty products.

Attracting Different Customer Segments is another significant benefit of product diversification. By diversifying your product range, you can appeal to different demographic groups and consumer interests. For example, a reseller specializing in tech gadgets might expand their offerings to include smart home devices, wearable technology, and gaming accessories. This broader range attracts tech enthusiasts with varying interests, from smart home aficionados to avid gamers. By catering to diverse customer needs, you enhance the likelihood of attracting and retaining a larger customer base.

Mitigating Risks associated with relying on a single product category is a key advantage of diversification. If your business is dependent on one type of product and market demand shifts or competition intensifies, you face a higher risk of revenue fluctuations. By offering a variety of products, you spread the risk across different categories, reducing the impact of market volatility on your overall business. For instance, if the demand for skincare products declines, the addition of haircare and makeup items provides alternative revenue sources, helping to stabilize your business performance.

Enhancing Overall Business Resilience through diversification helps you adapt to changing market conditions and consumer preferences. A diversified product range allows you to respond more effectively to trends and shifts in demand. For example, if a sudden trend emerges in eco-friendly beauty products, a reseller with a diversified inventory that includes sustainable options can quickly adapt and capitalize on this trend. Diversification ensures that your business remains flexible and resilient in the face of market changes, enabling you to sustain growth and profitability.

Leveraging Cross-Selling Opportunities is another benefit of product diversification. When customers purchase multiple products from your expanded range, you can increase the average order value and enhance customer satisfaction. For example, a beauty products reseller who offers skincare, haircare, and makeup items can create bundles or promotions that encourage customers to purchase complementary products. This not only boosts sales but also enhances the overall shopping experience for customers, driving repeat business and loyalty.

Product diversification is a strategic approach that helps resellers cater to a broader customer base, mitigate risks, and enhance business resilience. By expanding your product range, you attract different customer segments, reduce dependency on a single product category, and create multiple revenue streams. This approach supports long-term growth and stability, allowing your business to adapt to market changes and consumer preferences effectively. Through thoughtful diversification, you can strengthen your market position, increase sales opportunities, and build a more robust and resilient reselling business.

5. Building a Unique Selling Proposition (USP)

Creating a compelling Unique Selling Proposition (USP) is a fundamental strategy for differentiating your products in a competitive market. A well-crafted USP highlights the distinct attributes of your products and clearly communicates why customers should choose them over those offered by competitors. By defining what makes your products unique, you can enhance your brand's appeal, attract more customers, and foster long-term loyalty.

Identifying Unique Attributes is the first step in developing a strong USP. This involves pinpointing the specific features, benefits, or qualities that set your products apart from the competition. For example, a reseller of handmade crafts might focus on the artisanal quality and unique craftsmanship of their products. These attributes could include hand-made processes, exclusive materials, or bespoke designs that cannot be found in mass-produced items. Highlighting these unique aspects allows you to create a clear and distinct message that resonates with your target audience.

Communicating Customer Benefits effectively is crucial for a successful USP. Beyond merely listing unique features, your USP should articulate how these features translate into tangible benefits for the customer. For instance, a tech gadget reseller might emphasize how their products enhance productivity through advanced technology or superior ease of use. By demonstrating how your products solve specific problems or fulfill particular needs, you create a compelling reason for customers to choose your offerings over those of your competitors.

Targeting Specific Customer Segments can further refine your USP. Understanding the demographics, interests, and preferences of your target audience allows you to tailor your USP to resonate with their values and needs. For example, a fashion reseller who targets eco-conscious consumers might highlight the sustainable materials and ethical production practices of their clothing line. By aligning your USP with the values and desires of your target audience, you strengthen your connection with potential customers and enhance the relevance of your brand.

Differentiating from Competitors involves analyzing what your competitors offer and identifying gaps or opportunities for differentiation. Conducting a competitive analysis helps you understand how your products and brand can stand out in the market. For instance, if competitors offer similar products but lack exceptional customer service, your USP could focus on providing superior support and personalized service. This differentiation helps you capture market share and build a reputation for offering something distinct and valuable.

Leveraging Brand Storytelling is an effective way to enhance your USP. Sharing the story behind your products, such as the inspiration, craftsmanship, or mission, creates an emotional connection with your audience. For example, a beauty products reseller might share the story of how their products are formulated with natural ingredients sourced from local communities. This storytelling approach adds depth to your USP and helps customers form a stronger, more personal bond with your brand.

Consistent Messaging and Branding are key to reinforcing your USP across all customer touchpoints. Ensure that your USP is clearly communicated through your marketing materials, website, social media, and customer interactions. Consistent messaging helps build brand recognition and reinforces the unique qualities of your products. For example, a tech reseller might consistently highlight their commitment to innovation and cutting-edge technology in all promotional materials, creating a cohesive and recognizable brand identity.

Building a compelling Unique Selling Proposition (USP) is essential for standing out in a crowded market. By identifying unique attributes, communicating customer benefits, targeting specific segments, and differentiating from competitors, you create a strong and effective USP. Leveraging brand storytelling and maintaining consistent messaging further enhance your USP, making your products more appealing and memorable to customers. A well-defined USP not only attracts customers but also fosters brand loyalty and supports long-term business success.

Call to Action:
Identify and evaluate potential products for your reselling business.

Activity:
Create a list of three potential products and assess their viability using market research tools.

Chapter 3: Sourcing and Supplier Relationships

Tip: "Building strong relationships with reliable suppliers is key to maintaining product quality and consistency."

1. Finding Reliable Suppliers

Finding reliable suppliers is a fundamental aspect of building a successful reselling business. Establishing strong relationships with trustworthy suppliers ensures a consistent supply of high-quality products, which is crucial for maintaining customer satisfaction and business growth. The process of finding and vetting suppliers involves utilizing various resources and strategies to identify partners who align with your quality standards and business needs.

Utilizing Supplier Platforms is an effective way to connect with potential suppliers. Platforms such as Alibaba and Global Sources provide access to a vast network of manufacturers and distributors from around the world. These platforms allow you to search for suppliers based on specific product categories, read reviews, and compare prices. For example, a fashion reseller might use Alibaba to find a clothing manufacturer that offers competitive pricing and meets their quality criteria. By leveraging these platforms, you can streamline the supplier discovery process and gain access to a wide range of options.

Attending Trade Shows offers valuable opportunities for finding reliable suppliers and building personal relationships with them. Trade shows and industry events bring together suppliers, manufacturers, and resellers, providing a unique environment to explore product offerings, discuss terms, and assess potential partners face-to-face. For instance, a fashion reseller attending a trade fair can interact directly with clothing manufacturers, review sample products, and negotiate terms in person. This personal interaction helps in evaluating the reliability and credibility of suppliers more effectively than online interactions alone.

Conducting Thorough Research is essential for ensuring the reliability of potential suppliers. This involves verifying their business credentials, checking references, and reviewing their track record. For example, a tech gadget reseller should research a supplier's reputation by looking at customer reviews, industry ratings, and any history of complaints or disputes. By conducting due diligence, you can minimize the risk of partnering with unreliable suppliers and ensure that they meet your standards for product quality and business practices.

Requesting Samples before making bulk purchases is a prudent approach to evaluate the quality of products and confirm that they meet your expectations. Suppliers often provide sample products upon request, allowing you to assess factors such as material quality, workmanship, and adherence to specifications. For example, a home goods reseller might request samples of furniture items to inspect for durability and design before committing to a large order. Testing samples helps in making informed decisions and reduces the risk of receiving subpar products.

Negotiating Terms and Conditions is a crucial step in establishing a successful partnership with suppliers. Clear and favorable terms help in ensuring a smooth and mutually beneficial relationship. This includes negotiating aspects such as pricing, payment terms, lead times, and shipping costs. For instance, a beauty products reseller might negotiate bulk purchase discounts and flexible payment terms to optimize cash flow and reduce costs. Effective negotiation helps in securing better deals and aligning supplier terms with your business needs.

Building Strong Relationships with suppliers is key to maintaining a reliable and consistent supply chain. Foster open communication, provide timely feedback, and address any issues or concerns promptly. For example, a fitness equipment reseller who maintains regular contact with their suppliers and provides constructive feedback can build trust and ensure a more collaborative partnership. Strong relationships with suppliers contribute to better service, reliability, and support.

Diversifying Your Supplier Base can mitigate risks associated with dependency on a single supplier. By sourcing products from multiple suppliers, you reduce the impact of potential disruptions in the supply chain, such as delays or quality issues. For example, a tech reseller might work with several manufacturers to ensure a steady supply of products and avoid disruptions if one supplier faces challenges. Diversification enhances the resilience of your supply chain and ensures continuity in your business operations.

Finding reliable suppliers is a critical component of reselling success. By utilizing supplier platforms, attending trade shows, conducting thorough research, requesting samples, negotiating favorable terms, and building strong relationships, you can secure dependable partners who meet your quality standards and align with your business needs. Diversifying your supplier base further strengthens your supply chain and ensures a consistent supply of high-quality products, contributing to the overall success and growth of your reselling business.

2. Negotiating Terms and Prices

Negotiating favorable terms and prices with suppliers is a vital strategy for optimizing profitability and managing costs in your reselling business. Effective negotiation can lead to significant cost savings, improved cash flow, and stronger supplier relationships, all of which contribute to the overall financial health of your business. The negotiation process involves several key elements, including bulk purchase discounts, payment conditions, and delivery schedules.

Discussing Bulk Purchase Discounts is an essential aspect of negotiation that can directly impact your cost structure. Suppliers are often willing to offer discounts for large orders, which can reduce your per-unit cost and increase your profit margins. For example, a reseller of tech gadgets might negotiate a bulk purchase discount with a supplier to lower the cost of high-demand electronics. By leveraging the potential for high-volume sales, you can secure better pricing and enhance your competitive edge in the market.

Negotiating Payment Conditions is another critical component of supplier negotiations. Favorable payment terms can significantly improve your cash flow and financial flexibility. This includes negotiating extended payment deadlines, installment options, or deferred payments. For instance, a fashion reseller might request extended payment terms to align with their sales cycle, allowing them to pay for inventory after generating revenue from sales. By securing flexible payment conditions, you can better manage your working capital and reduce financial strain.

Discussing Delivery Schedules is crucial for ensuring timely receipt of products and minimizing disruptions in your supply chain. Negotiating delivery schedules that align with your inventory needs and sales patterns helps in maintaining optimal stock levels and meeting customer demand. For example, a home goods reseller might negotiate faster delivery times with a supplier to ensure that new products are available in-store promptly. Clear agreements on delivery schedules can enhance operational efficiency and customer satisfaction.

Establishing Long-Term Partnerships can provide additional benefits during negotiations. Building strong relationships with suppliers often results in more favorable terms and a higher level of trust and cooperation. For example, a beauty products reseller who consistently orders from the same supplier may receive better terms and priority treatment due to the established partnership. Long-term relationships can lead to improved support, preferential pricing, and greater flexibility in negotiations.

Conducting Market Research before entering negotiations helps you understand industry standards and competitive pricing. By researching pricing trends and competitor deals, you can enter negotiations with a clear understanding of what constitutes a fair and competitive offer. For instance, a tech gadget reseller who is aware of current market rates and competitor pricing can negotiate more effectively and secure better terms from suppliers.

Preparing for Negotiations involves identifying your key priorities and constraints. This includes understanding your budget limitations, desired pricing, and acceptable payment terms. By being well-prepared, you can approach negotiations with confidence and clarity. For example, a fitness equipment reseller might prepare a detailed list of negotiation points, including desired discounts and payment conditions, to facilitate a structured and productive discussion with suppliers.

Leveraging Volume and Frequency of orders can strengthen your negotiating position. Suppliers are often more willing to offer favorable terms if they see the potential for ongoing business and regular orders. For example, a home décor reseller who commits to frequent orders or higher volumes may be able to negotiate better pricing or terms based on the anticipated repeat business. Demonstrating a commitment to consistent orders can enhance your negotiating leverage.

In summary, negotiating favorable terms and prices with suppliers is a crucial aspect of managing costs and improving profitability in your reselling business. By discussing bulk purchase discounts, negotiating payment conditions and delivery schedules, establishing long-term partnerships, conducting market research, preparing thoroughly, and leveraging volume and frequency, you can achieve cost savings, enhance cash flow, and build strong supplier relationships. Effective negotiation not only contributes to your financial health but also supports the overall success and growth of your reselling business.

3. Quality Control and Assurance

Implementing rigorous quality control measures is essential for ensuring high product standards and achieving customer satisfaction. Quality control and assurance involve a systematic approach to monitoring and evaluating product quality at various stages of the supply chain. By prioritizing quality control, resellers can minimize the risk of returns and complaints, strengthen brand reputation, and build lasting customer trust.

Regular Inspections are a fundamental aspect of quality control. Conducting systematic inspections of products ensures that they meet established quality standards before they reach customers. For example, a home goods reseller might implement a routine inspection process where products are checked for defects, workmanship issues, and adherence to specifications. Regular inspections help in identifying and addressing quality issues early, preventing substandard products from entering the market.

Sample Testing involves evaluating a representative sample of products to assess their quality and performance. This method is particularly useful for verifying that products meet quality benchmarks and specifications. For instance, a tech gadget reseller might test a sample of electronics for functionality, durability, and compliance with safety standards. Sample testing provides valuable insights into product quality and helps in making informed decisions about large-scale orders.

Setting Clear Quality Benchmarks establishes the standards that products must meet to be considered acceptable. These benchmarks can include criteria related to materials, craftsmanship, performance, and safety. By defining clear quality benchmarks, resellers create a consistent quality standard that guides both suppliers and internal teams. For example, a fashion reseller might set specific quality criteria for fabric durability, stitching quality, and colorfastness to ensure that clothing items meet customer expectations.

Implementing Supplier Quality Agreements can formalize quality expectations and responsibilities. These agreements outline the quality standards that suppliers must adhere to and may include provisions for regular audits, sample testing, and corrective actions. For example, a beauty products reseller might establish a quality agreement with suppliers to ensure that cosmetics meet safety and efficacy standards. Supplier quality agreements help in aligning expectations and ensuring that products consistently meet quality requirements.

Conducting Post-Production Audits provides an additional layer of quality assurance. Audits can be performed at various stages of the production process, including after manufacturing and before shipping. For example, a home décor reseller might conduct a post-production audit to verify that products are free from defects and meet quality standards before they are dispatched to customers. Post-production audits help in identifying and addressing any quality issues that may arise during manufacturing.

Gathering Customer Feedback is an invaluable source of information for assessing product quality and identifying areas for improvement. By soliciting and analyzing feedback from customers, resellers can gain insights into product performance, durability, and overall satisfaction. For example, a fitness equipment reseller might collect feedback through customer reviews and surveys to identify common quality issues and make necessary adjustments. Customer feedback helps in continuously improving product quality and meeting customer expectations.

Establishing a Returns and Warranty Policy provides customers with confidence in the quality of products and offers a mechanism for addressing quality issues. A clear returns and warranty policy outlines the process for returning defective products and obtaining refunds or replacements. For example, a tech gadget reseller might offer a one-year warranty on electronics, allowing customers to return faulty items for repair or replacement. A well-defined policy enhances customer trust and supports a positive brand image.

Training Staff on Quality Standards ensures that employees involved in quality control are knowledgeable and effective in their roles. Training programs can cover aspects such as inspection techniques, quality benchmarks, and handling of defective products. For example, a home goods reseller might provide training for quality control staff on how to identify common defects and follow inspection procedures. Well-trained staff contribute to maintaining high quality standards and ensuring consistent product quality.

Implementing rigorous quality control measures is crucial for maintaining high product standards and ensuring customer satisfaction. By conducting regular inspections, performing sample testing, setting clear quality benchmarks, establishing supplier quality agreements, conducting post-production audits, gathering customer feedback, implementing a returns and warranty policy, and training staff, resellers can enhance product quality, reduce returns and complaints, and build a strong reputation for quality. Prioritizing quality control not only improves customer trust but also supports the overall success and growth of your reselling business.

4. Building Long-Term Supplier Relationships

Building and maintaining long-term relationships with suppliers is a strategic approach that provides numerous benefits, including consistent product quality, reliable supply chains, and improved business terms. Cultivating strong, long-term partnerships involves several key practices, including fostering mutual trust, maintaining open communication, and demonstrating reliability. These practices help in securing favorable terms, enhancing collaboration, and ensuring a steady flow of high-quality products.

Fostering Mutual Trust is at the core of any successful supplier relationship. Trust is built through consistent, transparent interactions and a commitment to fair business practices. For instance, a beauty products reseller might build trust by consistently honoring agreements and addressing issues honestly. This trust encourages suppliers to prioritize your business and offer more favorable terms. Demonstrating integrity and reliability in all dealings helps in establishing a solid foundation for a lasting partnership.

Consistent Communication ensures that both parties are aligned and informed about expectations, changes, and potential issues. Regular updates, meetings, and feedback sessions can facilitate effective communication. For example, a home goods reseller might schedule regular check-ins with suppliers to discuss product performance, address any concerns, and share market insights. Open communication helps in resolving issues promptly, aligning on goals, and maintaining a productive relationship.

Timely Payments are crucial for maintaining good relationships with suppliers. Paying invoices on time demonstrates financial responsibility and respect for the supplier's business operations. For example, a tech reseller who consistently pays suppliers according to agreed terms builds a reputation for reliability and earns goodwill. Timely payments can also lead to favorable credit terms, discounts, and priority service, enhancing the overall partnership.

Providing Constructive Feedback helps suppliers understand your needs and expectations better. Feedback on product quality, delivery performance, and service can lead to improvements and better alignment. For example, a fashion reseller might provide detailed feedback to a clothing manufacturer about product quality and design preferences. Constructive feedback fosters continuous improvement and strengthens the supplier's commitment to meeting your standards.

Collaborating on New Products can strengthen supplier relationships and create opportunities for innovation. Working together on product development, design, or exclusive offers can enhance the value of the partnership. For example, a beauty products reseller might collaborate with a supplier to create a new line of skincare products tailored to market trends. Collaboration not only expands your product offerings but also deepens the supplier's investment in your success.

Negotiating Favorable Terms is often easier with long-term partners. Suppliers who value the relationship are more likely to offer better terms, such as discounts, extended payment periods, or priority shipping. For example, a home décor reseller with a strong relationship with a supplier might negotiate better pricing or receive early access to new products. Strong relationships provide leverage in negotiations and can result in more advantageous business terms.

Supporting Supplier Development can enhance the overall quality of products and services. By offering support, such as sharing market insights or assisting with quality improvements, you contribute to the supplier's growth and success. For example, a tech reseller might help a supplier by providing feedback on product performance and suggesting enhancements. Supporting supplier development strengthens the partnership and fosters mutual growth.

Building Personal Connections can also play a significant role in strengthening relationships. Personal rapport and understanding the supplier's business culture can lead to a more collaborative and trusting relationship. For example, attending supplier events or engaging in informal conversations can help build personal connections and strengthen the partnership.

Monitoring Relationship Health regularly to ensure that the partnership remains mutually beneficial is essential. Assess the relationship periodically to identify any issues or opportunities for improvement. For example, a fashion reseller might conduct an annual review of their supplier relationships to evaluate performance and address any concerns. Regular assessments help in maintaining a healthy and productive partnership.

In summary, building long-term supplier relationships involves fostering mutual trust, maintaining consistent communication, ensuring timely payments, providing constructive feedback, collaborating on new products, negotiating favorable terms, supporting supplier development, building personal connections, and monitoring relationship health. By implementing these practices, resellers can secure reliable supply chains, achieve better business terms, and enhance product quality, ultimately contributing to the success and growth of their reselling business.

5. Diversifying Supply Chain

Diversifying your supply chain is a vital strategy for mitigating risks and enhancing the resilience of your reselling business. By avoiding over-reliance on a single supplier, you create a more robust supply chain that can better withstand disruptions. This approach involves sourcing products from multiple suppliers to ensure a consistent and reliable supply, even if one supplier encounters issues. Here's how diversifying your supply chain can benefit your business and strategies to implement it effectively:

Mitigating Risks is one of the primary benefits of supply chain diversification. Relying on a single supplier can expose your business to significant risks, such as supply interruptions, quality issues, or financial instability. By engaging multiple suppliers, you spread these risks and reduce the potential impact of any single supplier's problems. For example, a home décor reseller might source products from several manufacturers to avoid disruptions caused by production delays or supply shortages from one source.

Ensuring Continuity of Supply is crucial for maintaining smooth operations and meeting customer demands. Diversification helps ensure that you have alternative sources if a primary supplier cannot deliver. This is particularly important in industries where demand is volatile or supply chains are prone to disruptions. For example, a fashion reseller might have backup suppliers for popular clothing lines, ensuring they can continue to offer these items even if their main supplier experiences delays.

Enhancing Flexibility and Agility in your supply chain allows you to adapt quickly to changes in market conditions, consumer preferences, or supply chain challenges. Having multiple suppliers enables you to shift orders or adjust inventory based on availability and performance. For instance, a tech reseller might switch to a different supplier if a new product becomes available or if there are issues with their current supplier's delivery times.

Improving Negotiation Leverage with suppliers is another advantage of diversification. When you work with multiple suppliers, you can compare terms, prices, and quality, giving you more leverage in negotiations. This can lead to better pricing, improved terms, and higher-quality products. For example, a beauty products reseller might negotiate better discounts and payment terms by showing that they have multiple sources for their inventory.

Expanding Product Range is possible with a diverse supply chain, allowing you to offer a broader selection of products. By sourcing from different suppliers, you can access unique or exclusive items that differentiate your product offerings from competitors. For example, a home goods reseller might source eco-friendly products from one supplier and luxury items from another, catering to different customer segments.

Maintaining Quality Standards can be achieved through diversification by selecting suppliers who meet your quality requirements. Regularly evaluating and auditing suppliers ensures that all sources maintain consistent standards. For example, a fashion reseller might assess the quality of garments from each supplier and establish quality benchmarks to ensure that all products meet customer expectations.

Building Stronger Supplier Relationships with a diverse network of suppliers fosters collaboration and mutual support. By engaging with multiple suppliers, you can create a network of partners who understand your needs and are committed to your success. For example, a tech reseller might work closely with several suppliers to develop new products or improve existing ones, benefiting from their combined expertise and resources.

Reducing Dependence on Any Single Supplier minimizes the risk of severe disruptions if that supplier faces issues. This is particularly important in global supply chains where geopolitical or economic factors can impact availability. For example, a fashion reseller might source from both domestic and international suppliers to buffer against global supply chain disruptions.

Implementing Supply Chain Monitoring practices helps in maintaining oversight of your diverse network. Regularly track performance metrics, such as delivery times, quality issues, and inventory levels, to ensure that all suppliers meet your expectations. For instance, a beauty products reseller might use supply chain management software to monitor and evaluate supplier performance across different regions.

Contingency Planning is crucial in a diversified supply chain. Develop plans to address potential disruptions, such as alternative suppliers or emergency inventory strategies. For example, a tech reseller might establish contingency plans for high-demand periods, ensuring that they can quickly switch suppliers or ramp up orders to meet increased customer needs.

Call to Action:
Identify and establish relationships with at least three reliable suppliers.

Activity:
Draft a supplier evaluation checklist to assess potential suppliers based on quality, reliability, and terms.

Chapter 4: Marketing and Branding

Tip: "Effective marketing and a strong brand identity are crucial for standing out in a competitive market."

1. Creating a Brand Identity

Developing a consistent brand identity is a cornerstone of establishing a memorable and impactful presence in the market. A strong brand identity not only defines who you are as a business but also communicates your values, vision, and unique offerings to your target audience. Here's how you can create and maintain a compelling brand identity that resonates with customers and stands out in a crowded marketplace:

Defining Your Brand Values and Vision is the first step in building a brand identity. Clearly articulate what your business stands for and the vision you have for its future. This involves understanding your core values, mission, and goals. For example, a tech reseller might define its brand values around innovation, reliability, and exceptional customer service, aiming to be recognized as a leader in technological advancements and customer support.

Developing a Visual Identity that reflects your brand's essence is crucial. This includes designing a logo, choosing a color palette, and selecting typography that aligns with your brand values and appeals to your target audience. For instance, a tech reseller might opt for a sleek, modern logo with a color scheme that conveys sophistication and technological prowess. Consistency in visual elements across all platforms ensures that your brand is easily recognizable and memorable.

Crafting a Brand Voice and Messaging that resonates with your audience is essential for effective communication. Your brand voice should be consistent across all channels, including your website, social media, and marketing materials. For example, a tech reseller might use a professional yet approachable tone in its communications, emphasizing expertise and customer-centricity. This helps in building a coherent brand experience and engaging effectively with your audience.

Creating a Compelling Brand Story helps humanize your brand and create an emotional connection with your audience. Share the story behind your business, including its origins, mission, and the journey it has taken. For instance, a tech reseller might highlight its commitment to innovation and how it started with a passion for cutting-edge technology and a desire to provide exceptional service. A compelling brand story fosters trust and loyalty among customers.

Building a Professional Online Presence is crucial for reinforcing your brand identity. This includes developing a user-friendly and visually appealing website that reflects your brand's values and offers a seamless user experience. For example, a tech reseller's website might feature sleek design elements, intuitive navigation, and detailed product information, reinforcing its image as a leader in technology and customer service.

Implementing Consistent Branding Across Channels ensures that your brand identity is reinforced everywhere your business interacts with customers. This includes maintaining consistency in your visual elements, messaging, and tone across social media, email marketing, packaging, and customer service interactions. For example, a tech reseller might use the same logo, color scheme, and brand voice in all its marketing materials and customer communications to create a unified brand experience.

Leveraging Customer Feedback to refine and strengthen your brand identity is an ongoing process. Regularly gather feedback from customers to understand their perceptions of your brand and identify areas for improvement. For instance, a tech reseller might conduct surveys or analyze customer reviews to gauge how well its brand identity aligns with customer expectations and make adjustments as needed.

Aligning Brand Identity with Business Strategy ensures that your branding efforts support your overall business goals. Your brand identity should reflect your strategic objectives and help differentiate you from competitors. For example, a tech reseller's brand identity might emphasize its focus on innovation and cutting-edge technology, aligning with its strategy to be a leader in the tech industry.

Cultivating Brand Loyalty through exceptional customer experiences and consistent brand messaging fosters long-term relationships with your audience. Ensure that every interaction with your brand reinforces your values and enhances customer satisfaction. For instance, a tech reseller might offer personalized customer support, exclusive promotions, and engaging content to build a loyal customer base.

Monitoring and Evolving Your Brand Identity as your business grows is important for staying relevant and competitive. Periodically review your brand identity to ensure it continues to resonate with your target audience and reflects any changes in your business strategy. For example, a tech reseller might update its brand identity to reflect new technological advancements or shifts in market trends.

2. Developing a Marketing Strategy

Formulating a comprehensive marketing strategy is vital for effectively reaching your target audience and driving sales. A well-rounded strategy leverages a mix of online, offline, and social media channels to maximize your brand's visibility and engagement. Here's a detailed guide to developing a robust marketing strategy that will help you achieve your business goals:

1. Setting Clear Objectives: Begin by defining what you aim to achieve with your marketing efforts. Clear objectives might include increasing brand awareness, generating leads, boosting sales, or enhancing customer retention. For example, a fashion reseller might set an objective to increase online sales by 30% within the next six months through targeted marketing campaigns. Establishing specific, measurable, achievable, relevant, and time-bound (SMART) goals ensures that your strategy is focused and effective.

2. Understanding Your Target Audience: Conduct thorough research to understand your target audience's demographics, interests, and buying behaviors. This includes analyzing factors such as age, gender, location, income level, and lifestyle preferences. For instance, a fashion reseller might identify their target audience as young professionals aged 25-35 who are interested in affordable, trendy office wear. Tailoring your marketing messages and tactics to this audience will enhance your relevance and impact.

3. Utilizing Online Marketing Channels: Develop a robust online marketing plan that includes various digital channels to reach your audience effectively. Key online channels include:

- **Social Media Marketing:** Leverage platforms like Instagram, Facebook, Twitter, and LinkedIn to engage with your audience, share content, and promote products. For example, a fashion reseller might use Instagram to showcase new arrivals, run targeted ads, and collaborate with influencers to expand their reach.
- **Content Marketing:** Create valuable and relevant content to attract and engage your audience. This can include blog posts, videos, infographics, and eBooks. For instance, a home décor reseller might start a blog offering decorating tips and DIY projects to drive traffic and build brand authority.
- **Email Marketing:** Implement email campaigns to nurture leads, offer promotions, and maintain customer relationships. Personalize emails based on customer preferences and behaviors to increase engagement. For example, a beauty products reseller might send personalized product recommendations and special offers to subscribers.

4. Exploring Offline Marketing Channels: Complement your online efforts with offline marketing strategies to reach customers through different touchpoints. Key offline channels include:

- **Events and Trade Shows:** Participate in industry events, trade shows, and local markets to showcase your products and connect with potential customers. For instance, a fashion reseller might host pop-up shops or participate in local fashion fairs to gain exposure and engage directly with shoppers.

- **Print Advertising:** Utilize traditional media such as newspapers, magazines, and brochures to reach a broader audience. Ensure that print materials are visually appealing and include clear calls to action. For example, a tech reseller might place ads in tech magazines to attract enthusiasts and early adopters.

5. Implementing Social Media Strategies: Develop targeted social media campaigns to build brand awareness and drive engagement. Strategies might include:

- **Influencer Collaborations:** Partner with influencers and brand ambassadors who align with your brand values to reach their followers. For example, a fashion reseller might collaborate with fashion bloggers and Instagram influencers to promote new collections.
- **Interactive Content:** Create engaging content such as polls, quizzes, and live videos to interact with your audience and gather feedback. For example, a fitness equipment reseller might run a live workout session or a Q&A with a fitness expert on social media.
- **Paid Advertising:** Invest in paid social media ads to reach specific audience segments and drive targeted traffic to your website. For example, a beauty products reseller might run Facebook ads targeting users interested in skincare and beauty.

6. Monitoring and Analyzing Performance: Regularly track and analyze the performance of your marketing campaigns to assess their effectiveness. Utilize tools like Google Analytics, social media insights, and email marketing reports to measure key metrics such as website traffic, conversion rates, and engagement levels. For instance, a fashion reseller might analyze Instagram engagement rates and website analytics to evaluate the success of their campaigns and make data-driven adjustments.

7. Adapting and Optimizing Strategies: Based on performance data and market trends, continuously refine and optimize your marketing strategies. Experiment with different tactics, adjust your messaging, and explore new channels to improve results. For example, if a fashion reseller notices higher engagement with influencer posts compared to direct ads, they might shift more budget towards influencer partnerships.

8. Building Brand Loyalty: Focus on creating exceptional customer experiences and fostering brand loyalty through personalized interactions, exclusive offers, and consistent communication. Encourage customer feedback and leverage it to enhance your products and services. For instance, a beauty products reseller might offer a loyalty program with rewards and special discounts to retain existing customers and attract repeat business.

9. Leveraging Partnerships and Collaborations: Form strategic partnerships with other businesses or organizations to expand your reach and enhance your marketing efforts. Collaborations can include co-branded promotions, joint events, or cross-promotional campaigns. For example, a tech reseller might partner with a popular tech blog for sponsored content and product reviews.

10. Evaluating Market Trends and Competitors: Stay informed about industry trends and competitor activities to ensure your marketing strategies remain relevant and competitive. Analyze market shifts, emerging technologies, and competitors' tactics to identify new opportunities and threats.

3. Content Marketing and SEO

Utilizing content marketing and SEO is a highly effective strategy for driving organic traffic to your website and engaging with your target audience. This approach involves creating valuable, relevant content and optimizing it for search engines to increase visibility and attract potential customers. Here's a detailed guide on how to leverage content marketing and SEO for your reselling business:

1. Creating Valuable Content:

- **Understanding Your Audience:** Begin by identifying the interests, needs, and pain points of your target market. This will guide you in creating content that resonates with them and addresses their specific needs.
- **Content Types:** Develop a variety of content types to keep your audience engaged. For example, a home décor reseller could create blog posts, how-to guides, infographics, videos, and eBooks that offer decorating tips, DIY projects, and design inspiration.
- **Quality and Relevance:** Ensure that your content is well-researched, informative, and engaging. High-quality content builds trust with your audience and establishes your authority in your niche.

2. Implementing SEO Best Practices:

- **Keyword Research:** Conduct thorough keyword research to identify relevant terms and phrases that your potential customers are searching for. Use tools like Google Keyword Planner, SEMrush, or Ahrefs to find keywords with high search volume and low competition.
- **On-Page SEO:** Optimize your content for search engines by incorporating targeted keywords into key elements such as titles, headings, meta descriptions, and URL structures. For instance, a blog post about "DIY Home Decor Ideas" should include this phrase in the title, headings, and throughout the content.
- **Content Optimization:** Use keywords naturally within your content to avoid keyword stuffing. Ensure that your content is easy to read and provides value to your audience. Utilize internal linking to connect related articles and enhance user experience.
- **Image Optimization:** Include relevant images in your content and optimize them with descriptive alt text. This helps search engines understand the content of the images and improves accessibility.

3. Building Authority and Trust:

- **Expertise and Credibility:** Position yourself as an expert in your field by providing in-depth, well-researched content. For example, a home décor reseller could write comprehensive guides on seasonal decorating trends or sustainable home design.
- **Guest Blogging and Backlinks:** Contribute guest posts to reputable industry blogs and websites to build backlinks to your site. This not only drives traffic but also enhances your site's authority and credibility in search engines.

- **User Experience:** Ensure that your website provides a positive user experience with fast loading times, mobile responsiveness, and easy navigation. A well-designed site encourages visitors to stay longer and explore more content.

4. Promoting Your Content:

- **Social Media Sharing:** Share your content across social media platforms to reach a wider audience and drive traffic to your website. Tailor your social media posts to highlight key points and encourage engagement.
- **Email Marketing:** Include links to your latest content in your email newsletters to keep your subscribers informed and drive traffic to your site. For example, a home décor reseller might feature new blog posts in their monthly newsletter.
- **Content Distribution Networks:** Use content distribution networks (CDNs) and syndication services to expand the reach of your content. This can help you attract more visitors and increase brand visibility.

5. Analyzing and Measuring Performance:

- **Analytics Tools:** Use tools like Google Analytics and Google Search Console to track the performance of your content and measure its impact on organic traffic. Monitor metrics such as page views, bounce rates, and average time on page.
- **Adjusting Strategies:** Regularly review your content performance data to identify what's working and what needs improvement. Adjust your content strategy based on these insights to

better meet the needs of your audience and improve SEO results.

6. Engaging with Your Audience:

- **Comments and Feedback:** Encourage readers to leave comments and feedback on your content. Engage with them by responding to their questions and comments to build a sense of community and loyalty.
- **Surveys and Polls:** Use surveys and polls to gather insights from your audience about their preferences and content needs. This can help you tailor your content strategy to better align with their interests.

7. Staying Updated with SEO Trends:

- **Algorithm Changes:** Stay informed about changes in search engine algorithms and SEO best practices. Regularly update your content and SEO strategies to adapt to new trends and maintain your search rankings.
- **Industry News:** Follow industry news and updates to keep up with emerging trends and technologies in content marketing and SEO.

4. Social Media Marketing

Leveraging social media platforms is a powerful strategy for promoting products, engaging with customers, and building a community around your brand. Each social media platform offers unique opportunities to connect with your audience in diverse ways, enabling you to tailor your approach to the specific characteristics and preferences of each platform's user base. Here's a detailed guide to utilizing social media marketing effectively:

1. Selecting the Right Platforms: Choose social media platforms that align with your target audience and business objectives. Different platforms cater to different demographics and content types. For example:

- **Instagram** is ideal for visual content and engages users with photos, videos, and stories. It's particularly effective for industries like fashion, beauty, and home décor.
- **Facebook** offers a broad reach and versatile content options, including text posts, images, videos, and live sessions. It's beneficial for community building and customer interaction.
- **Twitter** is great for real-time updates, promotions, and customer service interactions.
- **LinkedIn** is suitable for B2B marketing and professional networking, making it ideal for tech and business-related products.

2. Crafting Engaging Content: Create content that resonates with your audience and encourages interaction. This includes:

- **Visuals and Videos:** High-quality images and videos capture attention and effectively showcase your products. For instance, a beauty products reseller might post tutorial videos demonstrating how to use new products.
- **Interactive Stories:** Use features like Instagram Stories and Facebook Stories to run polls, quizzes, and Q&A sessions. These interactive elements increase engagement and provide valuable insights into customer preferences.

- **User-Generated Content:** Encourage customers to share their experiences with your products and feature their content on your social media profiles. This builds trust and authenticity while leveraging social proof.

3. Running Social Media Campaigns: Develop and execute targeted social media campaigns to promote specific products, offers, or events. Strategies include:

- **Paid Advertising:** Utilize sponsored posts and ads to reach a broader audience and drive traffic to your website. For example, a fashion reseller might run Instagram ads targeting users interested in trendy office wear.
- **Influencer Partnerships:** Collaborate with influencers who align with your brand to reach their followers and enhance your credibility. A beauty products reseller could partner with beauty influencers for product reviews and recommendations.
- **Contests and Giveaways:** Organize contests and giveaways to boost engagement and attract new followers. Ensure the rules are clear and the prizes are appealing to your target audience.

4. Building a Community: Foster a sense of community by actively engaging with your followers and responding to their comments and messages. This includes:

- **Customer Interaction:** Reply to comments, messages, and reviews in a timely and personable manner. For instance, a tech reseller should address technical questions and provide helpful information.
- **Community Building:** Create and nurture a brand community by encouraging discussions, sharing

user-generated content, and hosting live events. For example, a home décor reseller might host a Facebook group where enthusiasts share decorating tips and ideas.

5. Analyzing Performance: Regularly monitor and analyze the performance of your social media efforts to assess their effectiveness and make data-driven improvements. Key metrics to track include:

- **Engagement Rates:** Measure likes, comments, shares, and overall interaction with your content.
- **Reach and Impressions:** Analyze how many users see your posts and how often.
- **Conversion Rates:** Track how social media interactions translate into website traffic, product purchases, or other desired actions.

6. Adapting Strategies: Use insights from your performance analysis to refine your social media strategies. Experiment with different content types, posting times, and promotional tactics to optimize results. For example, if a beauty products reseller notices higher engagement with Instagram stories compared to regular posts, they might increase the frequency of their stories.

7. Leveraging Trends and Hashtags: Stay current with social media trends and use relevant hashtags to increase your content's visibility. Participate in trending conversations and incorporate popular hashtags related to your products. For instance, a fashion reseller might use hashtags like #FashionTrends and #OOTD (Outfit of the Day) to reach a wider audience.

8. Providing Value and Education: Share valuable content that educates and informs your audience. This could include how-to guides, industry news, and expert tips. For example, a fitness equipment reseller might post workout tips and equipment usage advice to engage their audience and position themselves as a knowledgeable resource.

9. Integrating Social Media with Other Marketing Efforts: Ensure your social media strategy complements and reinforces your other marketing efforts. Cross-promote content, synchronize campaigns, and maintain a cohesive brand message across all channels.

10. Monitoring Competitors: Keep an eye on your competitors' social media activities to understand their strategies and identify opportunities to differentiate your brand. Analyze their content, engagement levels, and follower interactions to gain insights and inspire your own approach.

5. Email Marketing and Customer Retention

Implementing email marketing campaigns is a strategic and effective approach for nurturing leads, retaining customers, and enhancing overall business growth. Through regular and thoughtful communication, email marketing helps keep your brand top-of-mind, fosters customer loyalty, and drives repeat business. Here's a detailed guide on how to leverage email marketing for maximum impact:

1. Building an Email List:

- **Subscriber Acquisition:** Focus on building a high-quality email list by offering incentives such as discounts, free trials, or exclusive content in exchange for subscribers' email addresses. For

example, a fitness equipment reseller could offer a free eBook on workout routines to new subscribers.
- **Opt-in Forms:** Use opt-in forms on your website, landing pages, and social media to capture email addresses. Ensure that the sign-up process is simple and straightforward to encourage more people to subscribe.
- **Segmentation:** Segment your email list based on factors such as purchase history, interests, and engagement levels. This allows you to tailor your email campaigns to specific customer groups and deliver more relevant content.

2. Crafting Effective Email Campaigns:

- **Personalization:** Personalize your emails by addressing recipients by their first names and tailoring content based on their preferences and behavior. For example, a fitness equipment reseller might send personalized workout tips based on previous purchases or browsing history.
- **Valuable Content:** Provide valuable and engaging content in your emails. This could include industry news, how-to guides, product reviews, and exclusive offers. For instance, a beauty products reseller might include skincare tips and product recommendations in their newsletters.
- **Clear Call-to-Action (CTA):** Include clear and compelling CTAs in your emails to drive desired actions, such as making a purchase, signing up for a webinar, or visiting your website. For example, a tech reseller might include a CTA encouraging readers to explore new gadgets with a special discount.

3. Structuring Your Email Campaigns:

- **Newsletter Design:** Design visually appealing and mobile-friendly newsletters that reflect your brand identity. Use high-quality images, concise text, and clear headings to enhance readability and engagement.
- **Frequency and Timing:** Determine the optimal frequency and timing for your email campaigns based on your audience's preferences and behavior. For example, a fashion reseller might send weekly updates, while a home décor reseller might opt for bi-weekly emails.
- **Automation:** Implement email automation to streamline your campaigns and reach customers at the right time. Automated emails can include welcome messages, abandoned cart reminders, re-engagement campaigns, and post-purchase follow-ups.

4. Enhancing Customer Retention:

- **Exclusive Offers:** Reward loyal customers with exclusive offers, discounts, and early access to new products. This helps in showing appreciation and incentivizing repeat purchases.
- **Feedback Requests:** Use email campaigns to solicit feedback from customers about their experiences with your products and services. For example, a fitness equipment reseller might send a survey to gather opinions on recent purchases.
- **Educational Content:** Share educational content that adds value to your customers' lives, such as how-to guides, tutorials, and expert tips. This helps in building trust and positioning your brand as a helpful resource.

5. Monitoring and Analyzing Performance:

- **Metrics Tracking:** Monitor key email marketing metrics such as open rates, click-through rates, conversion rates, and unsubscribe rates. Use these insights to evaluate the effectiveness of your campaigns and make data-driven improvements.
- **A/B Testing:** Conduct A/B testing on various elements of your emails, such as subject lines, CTAs, and design layouts, to identify what resonates best with your audience and optimize performance.

6. Compliance and Best Practices:

- **Compliance:** Ensure compliance with email marketing regulations, such as the CAN-SPAM Act and GDPR, by including an unsubscribe option in every email and obtaining proper consent from subscribers.
- **Best Practices:** Follow email marketing best practices to maintain a positive relationship with your audience. Avoid spamming, respect privacy, and focus on delivering value to your subscribers.

7. Re-engaging Inactive Subscribers:

- **Re-engagement Campaigns:** Develop re-engagement campaigns to reconnect with inactive subscribers and encourage them to become active again. Offer incentives or personalized content to reignite their interest.

8. Customer Loyalty Programs:

- **Loyalty Rewards:** Implement a customer loyalty program and use email marketing to promote it. For example, a beauty products reseller might offer points for every purchase, which can be redeemed for discounts or free products.

9. Seasonal and Event-Based Campaigns:

- **Timely Promotions:** Create seasonal and event-based email campaigns to capitalize on special occasions, holidays, or industry events. For example, a fashion reseller might run a holiday sale campaign with exclusive discounts.

Call to Action: Develop a comprehensive marketing plan that includes content, social media, and email marketing strategies to effectively reach and engage your target audience.

Activity: Create a content calendar for the next month, outlining blog posts, social media content, and email campaigns. This will help you stay organized and ensure a consistent flow of engaging content across all channels.

Chapter 5: Sales Techniques and Strategies

Tip: "Effective sales strategies are about understanding customer needs and delivering value."

1. **Understanding the Sales Funnel**

Understanding the sales funnel is fundamental to optimizing your sales process and improving conversion rates. The sales funnel is a model that outlines the journey potential customers take from discovering your product to making a purchase. It typically consists of four key stages: Awareness, Interest, Decision, and Action.

1. **Awareness:**

    - **Objective:** At this stage, the goal is to make potential customers aware of your product or service. This involves attracting attention and generating interest through various marketing channels.
    - **Strategies:** Utilize content marketing, social media advertising, SEO, and public relations to increase visibility. For example, a tech reseller might use targeted ads on social media platforms and SEO strategies to reach users searching for new gadgets.
    - **Metrics to Track:** Track metrics such as website traffic, social media impressions, and brand mentions to gauge the effectiveness of your awareness efforts.

2. **Interest:**

    - **Objective:** Once potential customers are aware of your product, the focus shifts to nurturing their

interest and engagement. This stage involves providing valuable information and building a connection.
- **Strategies:** Offer detailed product information, engage with potential customers through email marketing, and provide educational content such as blog posts or webinars. For instance, a tech reseller might send informative emails about the features and benefits of their products and offer free eBooks or guides.
- **Metrics to Track:** Monitor email open rates, click-through rates, and engagement with your content to assess how well you are capturing and maintaining interest.

3. Decision:

- **Objective:** At this stage, potential customers are evaluating their options and deciding whether to purchase from you. The aim is to position your product as the best choice and encourage a purchase.
- **Strategies:** Provide compelling offers, showcase customer testimonials, and highlight competitive advantages. For example, a tech reseller might offer limited-time discounts or bundle deals to incentivize purchases and differentiate their products from competitors.
- **Metrics to Track:** Analyze conversion rates, cart abandonment rates, and the effectiveness of promotional offers to determine how well you are converting interest into decisions.

4. Action:

- **Objective:** The final stage of the sales funnel is where the customer takes action and completes the

purchase. Ensuring a smooth and seamless buying experience is crucial.
- **Strategies:** Simplify the checkout process, offer multiple payment options, and provide excellent customer support. For instance, a tech reseller should ensure that their website's checkout process is user-friendly and that customer service is readily available to address any last-minute concerns.
- **Metrics to Track:** Track completed sales, average order value, and customer feedback to evaluate the success of your sales process and identify areas for improvement.

Optimizing Each Stage:

- **Awareness Optimization:** Use data analytics to understand which channels drive the most traffic and optimize your marketing strategies accordingly.
- **Interest Optimization:** Personalize communications and follow up with leads to maintain engagement and address their specific needs.
- **Decision Optimization:** Implement A/B testing on offers and messaging to determine what resonates best with your audience and leads to higher conversion rates.
- **Action Optimization:** Regularly review and streamline your checkout process to minimize friction and ensure a positive customer experience.

Practical Example: Consider a tech reseller who wants to improve their sales funnel. They start by creating engaging social media content and targeted ads to drive awareness. Next, they follow up with detailed product information and special offers via email to generate interest. To facilitate decision-making, they showcase customer reviews and offer time-limited discounts. Finally, they ensure a smooth checkout process and offer prompt customer support to encourage the purchase.

2. Lead Generation Techniques

Effective lead generation is vital for driving potential customers into your sales funnel and setting the stage for successful conversions. Employing a variety of techniques can enhance your ability to attract and engage leads, ensuring a steady flow of prospects for your business. Here's a detailed look at some key lead generation strategies:

1. Search Engine Optimization (SEO): SEO is a fundamental technique for attracting organic traffic to your website. By optimizing your website's content, structure, and metadata with relevant keywords, you can improve your search engine rankings and increase visibility. For example, a reseller specializing in fitness equipment might use keywords such as "best home gym equipment" or "affordable workout gear" to drive targeted traffic to their site. High-quality content, such as blog posts, product reviews, and buying guides, can also help attract potential customers searching for related topics.

2. Pay-Per-Click (PPC) Advertising: PPC advertising, such as Google Ads, allows you to create targeted ads that appear in search engine results and on relevant websites. This method is effective for reaching potential customers who are actively searching for products or services similar to yours. For instance, a fashion reseller might run PPC campaigns targeting keywords like "trendy office wear" or "affordable business attire." By setting a budget and bidding on relevant keywords, you can drive highly targeted traffic to your landing pages and increase the chances of capturing leads.

3. Social Media Marketing: Social media platforms offer powerful opportunities for lead generation through targeted advertising and engaging content. Each platform has unique features that can be leveraged to connect with different segments of your audience. For example, a beauty products reseller might use Instagram to showcase new arrivals and run targeted ads aimed at users interested in skincare. By creating engaging posts, running contests, and using hashtags, you can increase your reach and encourage users to follow your brand and visit your website.

4. Content Marketing: Creating valuable and relevant content is a great way to attract and engage potential leads. Content marketing involves producing resources such as blog posts, eBooks, whitepapers, and videos that address the interests and needs of your target audience. For example, a home décor reseller might produce a series of blog posts on interior design tips and trends. Offering these resources in exchange for contact information, such as email addresses, can help you build a database of qualified leads interested in your products.

5. Email Marketing Campaigns: Building and nurturing an email list allows you to engage with potential leads directly. Email marketing campaigns can be used to send personalized offers, newsletters, and updates to subscribers. For instance, a tech reseller might send targeted emails to users who have shown interest in specific products, offering them exclusive discounts or early access to new releases. Effective email marketing helps keep your brand top-of-mind and encourages potential customers to take the next step in the sales process.

6. Lead Magnets: Offering lead magnets, such as free trials, samples, or downloadable resources, can incentivize potential customers to provide their contact information. For example, a fashion reseller might offer a free styling guide or discount on first purchases in exchange for email sign-ups. Lead magnets are an effective way to attract prospects and build a list of interested leads who are more likely to convert.

7. Webinars and Live Demos: Hosting webinars or live demonstrations can be an effective way to engage potential leads and showcase your expertise. For instance, a tech reseller might conduct a live demo of new gadgets, allowing participants to ask questions and see the products in action. These interactive sessions not only provide value to attendees but also help build trust and credibility with your audience.

8. Networking and Partnerships: Building relationships with other businesses or influencers in your industry can help generate leads through referrals and partnerships. For example, a fitness equipment reseller might partner with fitness trainers or health bloggers to promote their products. Networking at industry events and trade shows can also lead to valuable connections and opportunities for lead generation.

9. Landing Pages and Lead Forms: Designing optimized landing pages and lead forms is crucial for capturing leads effectively. Ensure that your landing pages are focused on a single call-to-action, with clear and compelling content that encourages visitors to take the desired action. For example, a home goods reseller might create a landing page for a special promotion, featuring a simple lead form for visitors to sign up for exclusive offers.

3. Effective Sales Pitches

Crafting effective sales pitches is essential for capturing the attention of potential customers and persuading them to make a purchase. A compelling sales pitch not only highlights the benefits of your products but also connects with the customer on a personal level by addressing their specific needs and pain points.

Understanding Customer Pain Points:

To create an impactful sales pitch, start by understanding the customer's pain points. These are the challenges or problems that your potential customers are facing and that your product or service can help solve. Conducting market research, customer interviews, and analyzing feedback can provide valuable insights into what customers are struggling with. For instance, if you are selling ergonomic office chairs, you might find that many customers experience back pain from prolonged sitting.

Crafting a Solution-Oriented Message:

Once you have identified the customer's pain points, craft a message that positions your product as the solution. Clearly articulate how your product addresses these issues and improves the customer's situation. For example, you might highlight that your ergonomic office chairs are designed with advanced lumbar support and adjustable features that reduce back pain and enhance comfort. Emphasize the specific benefits that align with the customer's needs, such as improved posture, increased productivity, and overall well-being.

Using Persuasive Language and Storytelling:

Incorporate persuasive language and storytelling techniques to make your sales pitch more engaging and memorable. Instead of just listing features, use stories or scenarios to illustrate how your product has positively impacted other customers. For example, share a testimonial from a customer who experienced significant relief from back pain after using your ergonomic chair. This approach helps potential customers visualize the benefits and relate them to their own experiences.

Highlighting Unique Selling Points:

Differentiate your product by highlighting its unique selling points (USPs) that set it apart from competitors. Explain what makes your product special and why it is the best choice for the customer. For instance, if your ergonomic chairs use premium materials or innovative design elements not found in other products, make sure to emphasize these aspects. Providing clear, concise information about why your product is superior can help sway customers in your favor.

Engaging with the Customer:

Engage with the customer during the pitch by asking questions and encouraging dialogue. This approach helps you tailor your pitch to their specific interests and concerns. For example, ask questions about their current office setup or any discomfort they are experiencing. Use their responses to further customize your pitch and address their specific needs. Building a conversational relationship helps in creating a more personalized and effective pitch.

Addressing Objections:

Anticipate and address potential objections that customers may have. Common objections might include concerns about price, product quality, or the suitability of the product for their needs. Prepare responses that reassure customers and provide solutions to their concerns. For example, if price is an objection, highlight the long-term benefits and cost-effectiveness of investing in a high-quality ergonomic chair that can prevent health issues and improve productivity.

Closing the Sale:

Conclude your sales pitch with a clear call to action that encourages the customer to take the next step. Whether it's making a purchase, signing up for a trial, or scheduling a follow-up meeting, make sure the customer knows what action to take and how to proceed. For instance, offer a limited-time discount or a special promotion to incentivize immediate action.

Following Up:

After delivering your sales pitch, follow up with the customer to address any additional questions and reinforce your message. A timely follow-up shows that you are attentive and committed to meeting their needs, which can help in closing the sale and building a lasting relationship.

4. Closing Sales and Overcoming Objections

Developing effective strategies to close sales and manage objections is crucial for converting potential customers into actual buyers. This process involves understanding common customer concerns and preparing well-thought-out responses that address these issues confidently.

Start by identifying common objections that customers might have. These objections can range from price and product suitability to concerns about quality or competitor offerings. For example, a beauty products reseller might encounter objections related to the safety of ingredients, product effectiveness, or price comparisons with other brands.

Once potential objections are identified, prepare clear and concise responses to address these concerns. Your responses should provide factual information and reassurances that alleviate customer doubts. If customers are concerned about product ingredients, for instance, prepare detailed information about the sourcing, benefits, and safety of these ingredients, and include testimonials from satisfied customers.

Handling objections with confidence is essential for convincing customers. This involves being knowledgeable about your product and its benefits and being prepared to address concerns without hesitation. Practice your responses to common objections until you can deliver them smoothly and confidently. For example, if a customer questions the efficacy of your beauty products, confidently share evidence from clinical studies or customer reviews that demonstrate product effectiveness.

Empathy plays a significant role in managing objections. Show that you understand and appreciate the customer's concerns. If a customer expresses hesitation about the price, acknowledge their concern and explain the value that your product offers. Use empathetic language to convey that you are on their side and are committed to finding a solution that meets their needs.

Supporting your responses with evidence can significantly enhance their credibility. Use data, testimonials, case studies, or demonstrations to back up your claims. For instance, a tech reseller might provide performance comparisons or customer success stories to address concerns about a product's performance or reliability.

Offering solutions rather than just countering objections directly addresses the customer's concerns. If a customer is worried about the initial cost of a product, suggest financing options, discounts, or bundled offers that can make the purchase more affordable. Providing practical solutions demonstrates flexibility and responsiveness to customer needs.

Active listening is crucial during objection handling. Fully concentrate on what the customer is saying and respond appropriately. This approach allows you to tailor your response more effectively. For example, if a customer is hesitant about a product's compatibility with their needs, listen to their specific requirements and address them with tailored solutions.

Throughout the sales process, reinforce your product's value proposition. Highlight the unique benefits and advantages that set your product apart from the competition. If a customer is considering multiple options, emphasize the unique features and benefits of your product that address their specific needs and concerns.

After addressing objections, guide the customer towards making a decision. Use closing techniques that reinforce the benefits and create a sense of urgency. Offer a limited-time discount or emphasize the benefits of acting now to encourage the customer to complete the purchase.

Ensure that the closing process is smooth and straightforward, making it easy for the customer to proceed.

Post-sale follow-up is important for ensuring customer satisfaction and addressing any additional concerns. After closing the sale, reach out to the customer to confirm their satisfaction and offer support if needed. This follow-up helps in building long-term relationships and encourages repeat business.

In summary, developing strategies to close sales and handle objections involves identifying common concerns, preparing effective responses, and approaching objections with confidence. By empathizing with customers, providing evidence, offering solutions, and reinforcing your product's value, you can overcome objections and successfully close sales. Effective objection handling not only increases your chances of converting leads but also fosters trust and long-term customer relationships.

Call to Action: Identify and implement at least three sales techniques to improve your conversion rates and enhance your overall sales process.

Activity: Practice crafting and delivering a sales pitch for one of your products, focusing on customer benefits and value propositions. This exercise will help you refine your approach and ensure you can effectively communicate the value of your products to potential customers.

Chapter 6: Customer Relationship Management

Tip: "The foundation of a successful business lies in building strong relationships with your customers."

1. **Understanding Customer Needs and Preferences**

Understanding your customers' needs and preferences is crucial for tailoring your offerings and enhancing their overall experience. This process involves gathering and analyzing data to make informed decisions about product selection, marketing strategies, and customer engagement.

Start by collecting data on customer preferences and buying behaviors. This can be achieved through various methods, including surveys, customer feedback forms, and analyzing purchase history. For instance, a reseller of fitness equipment might distribute surveys to their customer base, asking about their favorite types of workouts, preferred equipment features, and brand preferences. By analyzing this data, you can identify patterns and trends that will guide your inventory decisions.

Pay attention to customer pain points and challenges. Understanding what difficulties your customers face helps in developing products or solutions that address these issues directly. For example, if customers frequently express frustration with the durability of fitness equipment, you can focus on sourcing or developing products known for their robustness and longevity.

Leverage market research tools and analytics to gain deeper insights into consumer behavior. Tools such as Google Analytics, social media insights, and industry reports provide valuable information about market trends and customer preferences. A fitness equipment reseller might use these tools to track trending fitness activities or identify emerging customer needs, enabling them to adjust their product offerings accordingly.

Segment your customer base to better understand the different needs of various groups. Customer segmentation involves categorizing customers based on demographics, purchasing behavior, and preferences. For example, you might find that younger customers prefer high-tech fitness gadgets, while older customers favor more traditional equipment. Tailoring your product offerings and marketing strategies to these segments ensures that you meet the specific needs of each group.

Engage directly with your customers to gather qualitative insights. This can be done through interviews, focus groups, or social media interactions. For instance, hosting a focus group with regular customers can provide in-depth feedback on new product ideas or changes to existing offerings. Direct engagement helps in building stronger relationships and gaining a more nuanced understanding of customer needs.

Use feedback to continuously refine and improve your product lineup. Regularly review customer feedback and sales data to identify areas for improvement or new opportunities. For example, if customers consistently express interest in eco-friendly fitness equipment, consider expanding your product range to include more sustainable options. Adapting to feedback helps in staying relevant and responsive to customer demands.

Incorporate customer preferences into your marketing strategies. Understanding what resonates with your customers allows you to create targeted marketing campaigns that highlight features and benefits that are most important to them. For example, if your research shows that customers are particularly interested in the versatility of fitness equipment, focus your marketing efforts on showcasing how your products can cater to various workout routines.

Monitor industry trends and competitor offerings to stay ahead of the curve. By keeping an eye on what is happening in the market, you can anticipate changes in customer preferences and adapt accordingly. For instance, if you notice a growing trend in home fitness solutions, you can proactively stock products that cater to this demand.

2. Personalizing Customer Interactions

Personalizing customer interactions is a powerful strategy for enhancing engagement and satisfaction. By tailoring communication and marketing efforts to individual preferences and behaviors, you create a more meaningful connection with your audience, which can lead to increased loyalty and repeat business.

Begin by leveraging customer data to customize interactions. Collect information on customer preferences, purchase history, and browsing behavior through various channels such as website analytics, customer surveys, and CRM systems. For instance, a fashion reseller might track a customer's previous purchases and browsing history to tailor product recommendations specifically to their style and preferences. This data-driven approach allows you to deliver more relevant and engaging content to each customer.

Implement personalized email campaigns to foster a deeper connection with your customers. Use insights from your data to segment your email list and send targeted messages that address the interests and needs of different customer groups. For example, you might send special offers on seasonal fashion items to customers who have previously shown interest in similar products. Personalizing email content not only increases the chances of engagement but also demonstrates that you understand and value your customers' preferences.

Utilize personalized product recommendations on your website and in marketing materials. Based on a customer's browsing history or past purchases, suggest products that align with their interests. For instance, if a customer frequently views and buys athletic wear, display related items such as workout accessories or matching outfits on their homepage or in follow-up emails. This approach enhances the shopping experience and encourages customers to explore additional products that fit their tastes.

Engage in one-on-one interactions to build stronger relationships. This can be done through personalized customer service, where representatives use customer data to address inquiries and provide tailored solutions. For example, if a customer contacts support with a question about a previous purchase, a representative who is familiar with their purchase history can offer more relevant assistance and recommendations. Personalizing customer service interactions can significantly enhance satisfaction and foster loyalty.

Leverage social media to create personalized experiences. Engage with customers through personalized messages, respond to their comments, and recognize their contributions or feedback. For instance, if a customer shares a positive review or posts about your products on social media, acknowledge their support with a personalized thank-you message or offer a special discount. This level of engagement helps in building a community around your brand and strengthens customer relationships.

Incorporate personalization into your customer loyalty programs. Tailor rewards and incentives based on individual customer preferences and purchase behavior. For example, you might offer exclusive discounts on products that a customer frequently buys or provide early access to new collections based on their interests. Personalizing loyalty rewards enhances the perceived value of the program and encourages ongoing engagement with your brand.

Monitor and analyze the effectiveness of your personalization efforts. Track metrics such as engagement rates, conversion rates, and customer feedback to evaluate how well your personalized interactions are resonating with your audience. Use this data to refine your strategies and ensure that your personalization efforts continue to meet customer expectations.

3. Omni-channel Engagement

Offering a seamless experience across multiple channels is essential for providing a consistent and convenient customer journey. Omni-channel engagement ensures that customers can interact with your brand through their preferred platforms, whether it's social media, email, or your website. This approach enhances the overall customer experience by creating a unified and accessible presence across various touchpoints.

Start by integrating your communication channels to create a cohesive customer experience. Ensure that your brand's messaging, tone, and visual identity are consistent across all platforms, including your website, social media profiles, email campaigns, and customer service channels. For example, a beauty products reseller might maintain a consistent brand voice and aesthetic across Instagram posts, email newsletters, and their website to reinforce brand recognition and trust.

Leverage social media platforms to engage with customers and drive interactions. Use these platforms not only for marketing but also for providing support and gathering feedback. For instance, a reseller might showcase new product launches and promotions on Instagram while responding to customer inquiries and feedback through direct messages. This approach allows customers to engage with your brand in real-time and through their preferred social channels.

Implement a unified customer service strategy that spans all channels. Ensure that customer support is accessible via multiple touchpoints, such as live chat on your website, email, social media, and phone. For example, if a customer reaches out with a question about an order through social media, they should receive the same level of support and information as they would through other channels. This consistency in service helps in building customer trust and satisfaction.

Create a seamless shopping experience by integrating your online and offline channels. For instance, if you have a physical store, offer options like click-and-collect, where customers can purchase items online and pick them up in-store. Similarly, provide online return options for products bought in-store to enhance convenience. This integration helps in bridging the gap between different shopping experiences and meets customer needs more effectively.

Utilize data to personalize omni-channel interactions. By analyzing customer behavior across various channels, you can tailor your communications and offers based on their preferences and interactions. For example, if a customer frequently browses skincare products on your website and engages with related content on social media, you can send them personalized email promotions for skincare items they've shown interest in. This data-driven approach enhances the relevance of your communications and increases engagement.

Ensure that your marketing campaigns are coordinated across all channels to maintain a consistent message and avoid conflicting information. For example, if you are running a promotion, ensure that the details are aligned across your website, social media posts, and email campaigns. This coordination helps in avoiding confusion and ensures that customers receive a clear and unified message.

Monitor and evaluate the effectiveness of your omni-channel engagement strategy. Track metrics such as customer interaction rates, conversion rates, and feedback across different channels to assess the performance of your approach. Use these insights to refine your strategy and improve the overall customer experience.

4. Proactive Customer Support

Providing proactive customer support involves anticipating customer needs and addressing potential issues before they escalate. This approach goes beyond reactive problem-solving, focusing on identifying and mitigating issues before they affect the customer experience. By implementing systems and processes that enable timely and efficient support, you can significantly enhance customer satisfaction and loyalty.

Begin by establishing mechanisms for monitoring customer interactions and feedback. Utilize customer service tools and analytics to track common issues and emerging trends. For example, a technology reseller might use a ticketing system to categorize and prioritize customer queries, allowing them to identify recurring problems and address them proactively. This data-driven approach helps in pinpointing areas where additional support or improvements are needed.

Implement proactive communication strategies to keep customers informed and engaged. For instance, send out regular updates on order statuses, system maintenance schedules, or potential issues that may affect their experience. By keeping customers informed, you can manage their expectations and reduce the likelihood of frustration. For example, if a product is temporarily out of stock, proactively notify customers about the delay and provide alternative solutions or estimated restock dates.

Develop and maintain a comprehensive knowledge base that customers can access for self-service support. This resource should include frequently asked questions, troubleshooting guides, and detailed product information. By empowering customers to find solutions on their own, you can reduce the volume of support requests and improve overall satisfaction. For example, a technology reseller might provide detailed troubleshooting steps for common technical issues, allowing customers to resolve problems quickly without needing to contact support.

Train your support team to recognize and address potential issues before they become significant problems. Equip them with the tools and knowledge needed to provide timely assistance and resolve issues efficiently. For instance, ensure that customer service representatives are well-versed in the products and services you offer, enabling them to provide accurate information and solutions. Training should also emphasize the importance of empathy and proactive problem-solving in customer interactions.

Utilize automated systems and tools to enhance proactive support. For example, set up automated notifications for order updates, warranty expirations, or subscription renewals. Automation can help in managing customer expectations and ensuring that important information is communicated promptly. For instance, an automated system might send reminders for upcoming product maintenance or offer assistance with renewal options before the subscription period ends.

Encourage customer feedback and use it to refine your proactive support strategies. Regularly solicit input from customers about their support experiences and any areas where they feel additional assistance would be beneficial. Use this feedback to make data-driven improvements and adjust your support processes accordingly. For instance, if customers frequently request more detailed product information, consider enhancing your knowledge base or providing additional resources.

Monitor and evaluate the effectiveness of your proactive support efforts. Track metrics such as customer satisfaction scores, resolution times, and the frequency of recurring issues to assess how well your proactive strategies are performing. Use these insights to continuously improve your support processes and ensure that you are meeting customer needs effectively.

5. Feedback and Improvement

Encouraging customer feedback is essential for continuous improvement and maintaining high levels of customer satisfaction. Actively seeking and incorporating feedback helps you understand your customers' experiences, identify areas for enhancement, and ensure that your products and services align with their expectations.

Start by implementing various channels for collecting feedback. Surveys, reviews, and social media interactions provide diverse avenues for customers to share their opinions. For example, a home goods reseller might use post-purchase surveys to gather feedback on product satisfaction and customer service experiences. Offering incentives, such as discounts or entries into giveaways, can encourage more customers to participate in surveys and reviews.

Regularly monitor and analyze the feedback you receive. Use tools and platforms to aggregate and evaluate customer comments, ratings, and suggestions. For instance, analyzing patterns in feedback can reveal common issues or recurring requests. If customers frequently mention dissatisfaction with product packaging, this insight can prompt you to make necessary improvements.

Actively respond to customer feedback to demonstrate that you value their input and are committed to making improvements. Engage with customers on social media, reply to reviews, and address concerns promptly. For example, if a customer leaves a negative review about a product defect, a prompt and empathetic response can turn a negative experience into a positive one by offering a resolution or compensation.

Utilize feedback to drive product and service enhancements. Incorporate customer suggestions into your development processes and make iterative improvements based on their input. For instance, if customers suggest additional features for a product, consider these suggestions when planning future updates or product launches. This customer-centric approach not only improves your offerings but also fosters a sense of collaboration and loyalty.

Communicate changes and improvements based on feedback to your customers. Let them know how their input has influenced your business decisions and what actions have been taken to address their concerns. For example, if you've improved product quality based on feedback, highlight these changes in your marketing communications to showcase your commitment to customer satisfaction.

Establish a process for continuously collecting and integrating feedback into your business operations. Regularly review feedback data and update your strategies and processes accordingly. This ongoing commitment to improvement ensures that you remain responsive to customer needs and adapt to changing market trends.

Call to Action: Evaluate and enhance your current CRM practices to better understand and serve your customers, ensuring a more personalized and satisfying experience.

Activity: Create a customer journey map outlining key touchpoints and interactions to identify areas for improvement. This will help you visualize the customer experience and pinpoint opportunities for enhancing your CRM strategy.

Chapter 7: Optimizing Operations and Efficiency

Tip: "Efficiency is doing things right; effectiveness is doing the right things."

1. Inventory Management Best Practices

Implementing inventory management software is crucial for maintaining optimal stock levels and improving overall operational efficiency. Effective inventory management helps ensure that you have the right products available when customers need them, while also preventing issues like stock outs or overstocking.

1. Accurate Stock Tracking: Inventory management software enables real-time tracking of stock levels across multiple locations. By integrating with your sales channels, this technology provides up-to-date information on product availability, sales trends, and inventory movements. For example, a reseller might use the software to monitor stock levels of popular electronics, ensuring that they can fulfill customer orders without delays.

2. Demand Forecasting: Utilizing historical sales data and predictive analytics, inventory management software helps forecast future inventory needs. This forecasting capability allows you to anticipate demand fluctuations based on seasonal trends, market conditions, and promotional activities. For instance, a reseller might analyze past sales data to predict higher demand for certain products during holiday seasons, enabling them to stock up accordingly.

3. Automated Replenishment: Inventory management software can automate the reordering process, setting thresholds for minimum stock levels and generating purchase orders when inventory falls below these levels. This automation reduces the risk of stockouts and ensures timely replenishment. For example, if a reseller's software detects that stock levels of a bestselling item are running low, it can automatically place an order with the supplier to replenish inventory before it runs out.

4. Centralized Inventory Control: For resellers operating across multiple channels or locations, inventory management software provides a centralized view of stock across all platforms. This consolidation helps prevent overselling and ensures consistency in stock availability. For instance, a reseller with both an online store and a physical retail location can use the software to synchronize inventory levels, ensuring that customers receive accurate stock information regardless of their shopping channel.

5. Inventory Optimization: Analyzing inventory turnover rates and carrying costs with the help of inventory management software helps optimize stock levels. By identifying slow-moving items and adjusting inventory strategies, you can reduce carrying costs and improve profitability. For example, if the software identifies that certain products are not selling as quickly as expected, you can implement discount promotions or adjust ordering quantities to avoid excess inventory.

6. Integration with Other Systems: Integrating inventory management software with other business systems, such as accounting, sales, and customer relationship management (CRM) tools, enhances overall efficiency. This integration ensures that data flows seamlessly between systems, reducing manual data entry and improving accuracy. For instance, integrating inventory management with accounting software allows for real-time updates on inventory costs and financial reporting.

7. Reporting and Analytics: Inventory management software provides comprehensive reporting and analytics features, allowing you to generate insights into stock performance, sales trends, and inventory metrics. These reports help in making data-driven decisions and identifying areas for improvement. For example, you might use the software's reporting capabilities to analyze which products are performing well and adjust your inventory strategy accordingly.

8. Streamlined Returns Management: Managing returns efficiently is a key aspect of inventory control. Inventory management software can streamline the returns process by tracking returned items and updating stock levels accordingly. For instance, if a customer returns a product, the software can automatically adjust inventory levels and initiate a restocking process, ensuring that the item is available for future sales.

2. Streamlining Order Fulfillment

Automating order processing and fulfillment is essential for enhancing efficiency, minimizing errors, and speeding up delivery times. Integration with fulfillment services ensures a seamless flow from order placement to delivery, greatly improving operational effectiveness and customer satisfaction.

Integration with e-commerce platforms is a key component of streamlining order fulfillment. By connecting your online store with fulfillment services, orders are automatically transmitted to the fulfillment center, reducing manual entry and minimizing the risk of errors. This integration allows for a smooth transition of order information, ensuring that orders are processed quickly and accurately.

Automated order processing tools handle various tasks such as inventory checks, order verification, and packaging. Automation speeds up these processes and reduces the potential for human error. For example, an automated system can verify stock availability, generate packing slips, and initiate shipping, all without manual intervention, leading to faster and more reliable fulfillment.

Providing customers with real-time order tracking enhances transparency and improves their overall experience. Automated systems update customers on the status of their orders throughout the process, from processing to shipment and delivery. By sending automated updates, customers stay informed about their order's progress and estimated delivery time, which builds trust and satisfaction.

Efficient inventory management is another crucial aspect of streamlined order fulfillment. Integration with inventory systems ensures that stock levels are updated in real time as orders are processed. This prevents issues such as overselling or stock outs by keeping inventory information accurate and current. For instance, when an order is placed, the system automatically adjusts inventory levels to reflect the change.

Automated systems also optimize shipping and handling by generating shipping labels, selecting the best shipping methods, and managing delivery schedules. This automation improves accuracy and reduces delivery times. For example, the system might select the most cost-effective carrier based on the order's weight and destination, ensuring timely delivery and cost savings.

Reducing errors is a significant benefit of automating order fulfillment. Automated systems can cross-check order details, verify addresses, and ensure correct packing and shipping. By flagging discrepancies and preventing mistakes, automation enhances the accuracy of order fulfillment and reduces the likelihood of customer complaints.

Scalability is another advantage of automated fulfillment systems. As your business grows and order volumes increase, automated systems can handle the increased demand without compromising efficiency. This flexibility allows you to manage higher order quantities seamlessly, particularly during peak seasons.

Improved customer service is a direct result of efficient order fulfillment. Timely delivery and accurate processing enhance the overall customer experience. By reducing delays and minimizing errors, automation contributes to higher customer satisfaction, leading to positive reviews and repeat business. Leveraging Technology and Automation

Investing in technology and automation tools can significantly streamline your operations and enhance productivity. For instance, a fashion retailer might use an

AI-powered chat bot to handle customer inquiries efficiently. This not only frees up human resources for more complex tasks but also ensures quick and consistent responses to customer queries. Leveraging technology can improve operational efficiency, reduce costs, and enhance the overall customer experience.

Call to Action: Identify one area in your operations where you can implement efficiency improvements to enhance productivity and customer satisfaction.

Activity: Conduct a time-and-motion study of your order fulfillment process to identify bottlenecks and areas for improvement. This analysis will help you understand where delays occur and how to streamline operations for better efficiency.

Chapter 8: Financial Management and Profitability

Tip: "Profitability is not just about revenue; it's about managing costs and maximizing margins."

1. Budgeting and Financial Planning

Developing a comprehensive budget is essential for managing finances effectively and supporting business growth. A well-structured budget provides a roadmap for forecasting revenue, controlling expenses, and ensuring that financial resources are allocated in alignment with business goals.

To start, it's important to forecast revenue based on realistic sales projections. This involves analyzing past sales data, market trends, and economic conditions to estimate future income. For instance, a reseller might use historical sales data to project future revenue, taking into account seasonal fluctuations and market demand. Accurate revenue forecasting helps in setting achievable financial goals and planning for various business needs.

Expense management is a key component of budgeting. Categorizing expenses into fixed costs (such as rent and salaries) and variable costs (such as inventory and marketing) allows you to monitor and control spending more effectively. For example, a reseller could track monthly expenses related to product procurement, marketing campaigns, and operational overheads. By identifying areas where expenses can be reduced or optimized, you can improve profitability and maintain financial health.

Cash flow projections are vital for ensuring that you have sufficient funds to cover operational costs and investments. Creating a cash flow forecast involves estimating when money will come in (revenue) and when it will go out (expenses). For instance, a reseller might project cash flow to ensure that funds are available for paying suppliers, covering payroll, and investing in marketing. Monitoring cash flow helps in avoiding shortages and planning for future financial needs.

Allocating funds strategically is crucial for supporting various aspects of your business. This includes setting aside resources for marketing efforts, operational improvements, and growth initiatives. For example, a reseller might allocate a portion of their budget to digital marketing campaigns, technological upgrades, and new product lines. Strategic allocation ensures that all areas of the business receive the necessary support to achieve objectives and drive growth.

Regularly reviewing and adjusting your budget is important for staying on track with financial goals. As market conditions and business needs change, it's essential to update your budget to reflect these changes. For instance, if a reseller experiences unexpected changes in sales volume or incurs additional costs, they should adjust their budget accordingly. Regular reviews allow you to make informed decisions and respond proactively to financial challenges.

Incorporating contingency planning into your budget helps in preparing for unforeseen expenses and economic uncertainties. Setting aside a contingency fund for emergencies or unexpected costs ensures that you can handle financial surprises without disrupting your operations. For example, a reseller might establish a reserve fund to cover unexpected inventory shortages or equipment repairs.

Utilizing financial planning tools and software can enhance the accuracy and efficiency of budgeting. Tools such as spreadsheets, financial planning software, and accounting systems help in tracking expenses, analyzing financial data, and generating reports. For instance, a reseller might use financial software to automate budget tracking and generate real-time financial reports. These tools provide valuable insights and support informed decision-making.

By focusing on these aspects of budgeting and financial planning, you can create a solid financial foundation for your business. Accurate forecasting, effective expense management, strategic allocation, and regular reviews contribute to financial stability and support your long-term business objectives. Proper budgeting not only helps in maintaining control over finances but also enables you to make informed decisions that drive growth and ensure the success of your business.

2. Cash Flow Optimization

Implementing effective cash flow management strategies is essential for maintaining liquidity and meeting financial obligations. This involves managing the timing of incoming and outgoing cash flows to ensure that your business always has enough cash on hand to cover its expenses. For example, a reseller might negotiate favorable payment terms with suppliers to delay outflows and optimize cash flow. By keeping a close eye on your cash flow, you can avoid liquidity issues and ensure the smooth operation of your business.

3. Cost Control and Expense Management

Identifying cost-saving opportunities and implementing cost control measures can significantly enhance your profitability. This might involve renegotiating supplier contracts, reducing unnecessary expenses, or finding more efficient ways to operate. For example, a reseller might renegotiate supplier contracts to lower procurement costs. By regularly reviewing your expenses and seeking ways to cut costs without compromising quality, you can improve your bottom line and invest more resources into growth initiatives.

4. Pricing Strategy and Profit Margins

Developing a competitive pricing strategy is key to maximizing profit margins while remaining attractive to customers. This involves analyzing market trends, understanding customer demand, and setting prices that balance competitiveness with profitability. For instance, a tech reseller might adjust prices dynamically based on market conditions to stay competitive and maximize profits.

5. Financial Performance Analysis

Monitoring key financial metrics is vital for assessing your business's performance and financial health. Using financial analytics tools, you can analyze trends, identify strengths and weaknesses, and make data-driven decisions. For example, a reseller might use these tools to track sales performance, profit margins, and expense ratios. Regular financial performance analysis helps you stay informed about your business's financial status and make proactive adjustments to improve outcomes.

Call to Action: Review your financial management practices and identify areas for improvement to enhance your business's financial health and stability.

Activity: Conduct a financial health assessment to evaluate liquidity ratios, profitability margins, and financial leverage metrics. This assessment will provide valuable insights into your business's financial strengths and weaknesses, helping you make informed decisions to support long-term success.

Chapter 9: Scaling Your Reselling Business

Tip: "Scaling isn't just about growing bigger; it's about growing smarter and sustaining success."

1. Market Expansion Strategies

Identifying new target markets, geographic regions, or customer segments is a crucial step in expanding your market reach. This involves researching and analyzing potential markets to determine where your products can gain traction. For example, a tech reseller might explore international markets to expand their customer base, tapping into regions with growing demand for technology products. By identifying and entering new markets, you can diversify your revenue streams and reduce dependence on a single market.

2. Diversifying Product Portfolio

Expanding your product offerings to cater to evolving customer preferences and market demands can help attract a broader customer base. This strategy involves introducing complementary product lines that align with your existing offerings. For instance, a beauty products reseller might diversify by introducing skincare and haircare products to complement their makeup line. By continuously evolving your product portfolio, you can meet the changing needs of your customers and stay competitive in the market.

3. E-commerce and Digital Transformation

Investing in e-commerce platforms and digital marketing initiatives is essential for broadening your market access and reaching more customers. Enhancing your online presence through a user-friendly website, effective SEO strategies, and targeted digital marketing can significantly boost your visibility and sales. For example, a fashion retailer might enhance their online presence by optimizing their website for mobile users and employing social media advertising. Embracing digital transformation helps you stay relevant in the increasingly online-oriented marketplace.

4. Operational Scalability and Infrastructure

Strengthening your operational capabilities and supply chain logistics is crucial for supporting increased sales volume and ensuring smooth operations. Implementing scalable technologies and efficient logistics solutions can streamline your processes and handle growing demand effectively. For instance, a home goods reseller might implement scalable technologies such as automated inventory management systems to improve efficiency. By enhancing your infrastructure, you can maintain high service levels and support sustainable growth.

5. Strategic Partnerships and Alliances

Forming strategic partnerships and alliances can amplify your market reach and leverage shared resources for mutual benefit. Collaborating with other businesses, influencers, or organizations can help you access new customer segments and enhance your brand's credibility. For example, a fitness equipment reseller might partner with gyms and fitness influencers for co-marketing campaigns, reaching a larger audience and boosting brand awareness. Strategic partnerships can provide valuable opportunities for growth and innovation.

Call to Action: Assess your readiness for scaling and identify one growth opportunity to prioritize, ensuring you are well-prepared to expand your market reach effectively.

Activity: Conduct a SWOT analysis to evaluate your internal capabilities, market opportunities, competitive landscapes, and potential risks. This analysis will help you identify your strengths, weaknesses, opportunities, and threats, providing a comprehensive understanding of your growth potential and areas to focus on.

Conclusion

Success in reselling is a journey of continuous learning, adapting, and growing. Reflect on the strategies and insights shared in this book and consider how you can implement these practices to enhance your business. Stay flexible, keep learning, and be ready to adapt to the evolving market landscape. Your dedication to excellence and customer satisfaction will be the driving forces that propel your reselling business to new heights.

By staying committed to ongoing improvement and innovation, you position your business to thrive in a competitive environment. Embrace new opportunities, set ambitious goals, and continually strive for excellence. The reselling industry is dynamic, and those who are willing to learn and adapt are the ones who will succeed.

Sayed Aris Khelwati
11:48 AM – Aug 01 2024
Halifax, NS, Canada

www.ingramcontent.com/pod-product-compliance
Lightning Source LLC
Chambersburg PA
CBHW071836210526
45479CB00001B/162